An Asperger's Guide to Entrepreneurship

An Asperger's Guide to

Entrepreneurship

Setting Up Your Own Business for
Professionals with Autism Spectrum Disorder

Rosalind A. Bergemann
Foreword by Michael John Carley

Jessica Kingsley *Publishers*
London and Philadelphia

First published in 2015
by Jessica Kingsley Publishers
73 Collier Street
London N1 9BE, UK
and
400 Market Street, Suite 400
Philadelphia, PA 19106, USA

www.jkp.com

Library of Congress Cataloging in Publication Data
A CIP catalog record for this book is available from the Library of Congress

British Library Cataloguing in Publication Data
A CIP catalogue record for this book is available from the British Library

ISBN 978 1 84905 509 3
eISBN 978 0 85700 978 4

Printed and bound in Great Britain

This book is dedicated to all those outstanding individuals on the autism spectrum who have either taken the step to become professionals within their own companies, or are on the journey to doing so.

It is also dedicated to my daughter Dawn, who continues to inspire, motivate and encourage me every day!

Contents

Foreword

The unemployment crisis in the developed world is well known, if not felt; and part of the reason why we're so well-informed is that labor research focuses much of its efforts on the jobless – their percentages, and the wide-ranging sociological consequences of their dilemma. But almost no research has ever gone into the realm of employee dissatisfaction, especially when it comes to the percentage of the workforce that is diagnosed along the autism spectrum. Granted, spectrum or not, getting study participants to be honest about how dissatisfied they are in existing jobs would be a tough task for any researcher – no one wants to tick off their employers with traceable comments that, in a tough job market, could lead to the employee's dismissal. But still, the near-absence of any real, quantifiable information herein is surprising.

Thanks to such a shortage of information, we do not know for certain that millions are dissatisfied with their existing jobs; yet in our hearts, we *do* (know this to be true). And fellow spectrumites are perhaps even more at risk herein. We feel stuck in unwanted jobs for many possible reasons – the corporate atmosphere that relies so heavily on socialization, the sensory demands of the office itself, the lack of interest in our company's products, the frustration of a boss whose intelligence doesn't measure up to ours; or any of the thousands of other elements I can think up (including the aforementioned shortage of open positions to transition towards, which affects everyone). But our spectrum uncertainty also adds to our fears – the risk factor of leaving, if not embarking on a business of our own feels infinitely heavier to us due to our lack of social confidence (one could argue that our ideal job is anthropologist, as we are destined to labor proportionately harder when learning 'how the world works'). No matter how good we are at what we do – and in the right positions we are *very* good – our capacity for feeling 'stuck' seems higher.

Adding to this malaise is the knowledge that too many of us would probably fare much better in a start-up; a business designed around a special interest that feeds our heightened capacity for passionate focus, and that we run as *we* see fit. We know we'd be great in this role, but we justifiably wonder if we're being delusional, if we're in denial, or just that we don't fully know what we need in order to make this dream come true.

Today, the word 'entrepreneurship' is hot. Stories of billion-dollar start-ups fill the business sections of our newspapers, and lifestyle articles often chronicle the journey that the single mother took to create a web-based business that, while paying less than a phone app purchased by Google or Facebook, has given her a steady income and the flexible hours to care for her child. These stories, combined with a record-high dissatisfaction with the corporate world have now embedded entrepreneurship in our psyches not as the fluke, fringe alternative to a 'real job' that it was once thought to be; but now as perhaps a last, imperative resort, if not an exciting new path. The myth that you need an MBA to create a successful business is gone, and 'the powerful few' are infinitely less on the lookout for conformists, and more so for entrepreneurial spirit, as well as the outside the box thinking that the autism spectrum can so often produce. Silicon Valley (a town I half-joke that we spectrumites built) has taught the world a lot.

Granted, the odds of a start-up succeeding are small – maybe even as small as making it as an actor in New York or London. But should a start-up fail, a new start-up can emerge, this time with the added knowledge and experience to give the new creation a better chance of success than the previous attempt. And as an entrepreneur your only requirement is to find something you really want to do, making sure it can be successful (keeping in mind that nothing is foolproof), and then you make it successful. There will be lots to learn, yes; but the spectrum mind is well suited to this task. We can be sponges when it comes to information that we want to learn.

But what do we *need* to learn? And *in what order* do we need to implement all the things we'll need to learn? Where are all the sources we'll need to find the things we need to learn? What's different about an Asperger entrepreneur as opposed to a neurotypical entrepreneur? And what about all the things *we might miss in our research, yet will need badly down the road?*

Enter Rosalind Bergemann's *An Asperger's Guide to Entrepreneurship.*

Not only is a book on Asperger entrepreneurship long overdue, but Rosalind may have shut down the need for future books on the subject. She has written a thoroughly complete, easy-to-read guide that will satisfy not just the budding entrepreneur who has some idea of what's required, but also the dreamer who has no clue where to start.

Her book is so comprehensive that based on the reader's business ideas, not all the information herein will be needed – whole passages could be skipped. But that's a good thing, not a bad thing, as it means that everyone's business ideas have been fully catered to within these pages; whether said reader wishes to start a solo consulting firm, or a business that eventually has them managing hundreds of employees. From contracts, networking options, and personal leadership development, to an extensive checklist and toolkit Rosalind has devised, there is little chance that something required for an audience members' business idea will not be found. It is that good a book.

Rosalind herself is the perfect author for such a book. 'One of us', Rosalind has had a career in the business world that few of our folks have attained (though thanks to her book, the odds may dramatically increase), as a past Finance Director, Operations Director, Managing Director, Human Resources Director, Management Consultant, and for having existed as the President and CEO of Globalite Management Services Limited the last dozen years...You get the picture.

In the spectrum world we have seen too many books about employment written by spectrum authors who, paradoxically, have had great difficulty holding a job down (lots of good information on what *not* to do when seeking or maintaining a job, but very little in the 'what to do' department). Rosalind is the ultimate spectrumite to write such a book.

An Asperger's Guide to Entrepreneurship had me exclaiming 'Finally!' too many times as I read it. It promises *real* hope, and positive change in the lives of so many of us. The surprising answer to what usually leads one out of the debilitating 'stuck' feelings, and into a satisfaction with our lives that we might not have even known could exist, is desire, effort, and continued momentum. With start-ups we are not waiting for others to come to our rescue, or for 'the phone to ring'. With start-ups, there is something we can do to control our own destiny.

Rosalind has done her bit. So the ball's in our court now. Let's show people what we can do with this relatively new, emotionally-healthy option for employment...if not, at the very least, enjoy our lives a whole lot more.

Michael John Carley

Founder of GRASP, and the author of *Asperger's From the Inside-Out: A Supportive and Practical Guide for Anyone with Asperger's Syndrome*

Acknowledgements

Acknowledgements are initially due to all the remarkable fellow Aspergerians I have had the privilege of liaising with as a result of my work with the organisation Asperger Leaders.

Particular thanks are given to those people who have added to the insights in this book through their valuable contributions: Allison Bruning, CEO/Founder: Mountain Springs House; Dan Coulter, President: Coulter Video Inc.; Scott Sheinfeld, Founder: Infected Sloths LLC; Jeremy Samson, Managing Director: Time2Train. In addition, those contributors who have chosen to remain partially anonymous, namely Alex: Entrepreneur from the USA; David H.: Entrepreneur from London; Simon: Entrepreneur from Australia; Gwyneth: Entrepreneur from the UK; Scott: Entrepreneur from USA; Aaron: Entrepreneur from Australia; Ross: Entrepreneur from the UK; James: Entrepreneur from New Zealand; Denise: Entrepreneur from South Africa; Patrick: Entrepreneur from UK; John: Entrepreneur-to-be from Ireland. Additional acknowledgement and thanks to the several contributors who preferred to contribute anonymously. Although I cannot acknowledge you personally, I hope you know how valuable your comments were.

Introduction

As a professional with Asperger syndrome, it is highly likely that you have spent many years developing strategies to be successful in the workplace, to overcome any challenges your Asperger's may present you, and utilising those qualities which tend to be strongest in those people with Asperger's. The emphasis here is that this is something we have always had to work at. I have heard it said that for those of us on the autism spectrum, operating in the workplace is like working in a different country with a completely different culture that we have never had explained to us, but that we need to operate within anyway. I prefer another, perhaps more radical, analogy. When I think about how I have developed my career within the neurotypical work environment, I tend to compare it to working in an alien world, all the while pretending to be an alien myself, since showing myself to be a homo sapiens rather than an alien would result in me being permanently 'alienated' (please excuse the pun!).

I am certain that if you are an individual with Asperger syndrome (or what is more broadly classified as an Autism Spectrum Disorder or ASD) who has been in the neurotypical work environment, you will probably find yourself nodding at this analogy, recalling instances when you have felt completely set apart from the people and company you work with and for, often for reasons that you really did not understand.

Learning to be successful in the business world despite this challenge is – in itself – often a very inspirational experience for many of us. We are overcoming that hindrance, and often excelling despite it. But sometimes this can be demotivating largely because of the fact that we are *always* having to fit in, always working to ensure we do things the neurotypical way, always putting in that extra effort to ensure we have not made a slip in any of our challenging areas. Another area in which we often feel frustrated is that we frequently have a great deal more insight into our areas of expertise than most neurotypicals, purely due to the way our minds work. We process information differently, collecting far more data than most people do, and as a result we frequently are far better able to analyse the situation at hand and come up with creative solutions. Often this is something that we are not able to explicitly explain. It is just something that we are able to do – and we are aware of the fact that we do this successfully.

However, when you work in the corporate world – which is effectively neurotypical in its mode of functioning – corporate constraints often result in ideas and concepts that cannot be explained or detailed in a fashion acceptable to the neurotypical group-think being disregarded or resisted. For those of us with the vision to see opportunities or threats so clearly, this inability to be able to act on what we see, develop or forecast is incredibly frustrating.

At the same time, there can be those individuals with ASDs who do very well within their organisations, but simply grow tired of constantly having to adapt – to be the malleable square peg that needs to contort to fit into the round hole. They recognise that they are good at what they do, and start to consider what it would be like not be accountable to the neurotypical corporate animal, but to develop a company that fits them instead.

Becoming an entrepreneur requires a lot of key skills such as knowledge of your market, understanding of your product or service, understanding of the competition, and so forth. However, more important are the personality traits that are required. These include determination, dedication, an ability to think outside the box, the ability to see detail where others can't, and the dedication to put in the time and effort necessary to make the business a success. Without these personality traits, a new entrepreneur is unlikely to succeed, no matter how great a businessperson they were in the corporate world. Fortunately for those of us on the spectrum, these tend to be personality traits that we do have, and we often reflect them very powerfully. People on the autism spectrum are dedicated to the point of obsession in some cases, and their tenacity is what can make a business incredibly successful.

That said, there are a number of areas essential for successful entrepreneurship that we are not naturally strong in, such as customer relations, networking and hiring, managing, and working with staff. We may not be naturally inclined to these areas, but with the correct information and development tools, these are areas in which you can be successful.

Before I continue with this introduction, I think it is relevant here to mention terminology used within the book. For many of us, we have been diagnosed as having Asperger syndrome. This name has its origin from the person who first recognised and wrote about the syndrome, Hans Asperger, in the 1940s. Asperger's work was not of particular interest at the time, but there was a resurgence of interest in his work in the 1980s, and the term Asperger's syndrome (or Asperger's disorder) was named after him posthumously, only in 1994 being officially recognised in the Diagnostic and Statistical Manual of Mental Disorders (DSM), published by the American Psychiatric Association.

The DSM was created to enable mental health professionals to communicate using a common diagnostic language and standard criteria for the classification of mental disorders. It was first published in 1952, but because our understanding of mental health is evolving, the DSM is periodically updated. In each revision, mental health conditions that are no longer considered valid are removed, while newly defined conditions are added. In 2013, the fifth edition of DSM was issued.

One of the most important changes in the fifth edition of the *Diagnostic and Statistical Manual of Mental Disorders* (DSM-5) (American Psychiatric Association 2013) is to autism spectrum disorder (ASD). The revised diagnosis represents a new, more accurate, and medically and scientifically useful way of diagnosing individuals with autism-related disorders.

Using DSM-IV, patients could be diagnosed with four separate disorders: autistic disorder, Asperger's disorder, childhood disintegrative disorder, or the catch-all diagnosis of pervasive developmental disorder not otherwise specified. Researchers found that these separate diagnoses were not consistently applied across different clinics and treatment centres. Anyone diagnosed with one of the four pervasive developmental disorders (PDD) from DSM-IV should still meet the criteria for ASD in DSM-5 or another, more accurate DSM-5 diagnosis. While DSM does not outline recommended treatment and services for mental disorders, determining an accurate diagnosis is a first step for a clinician in defining a treatment plan for a patient.

In line with the above changes, this book is intended to apply to all people who fall within the category of autism spectrum disorder (ASD), as defined in the DSM-5, including those of us who have previously been diagnosed as having Asperger syndrome. This in no way detracts from our unique contributions as Asperger professionals, but seeks to ensure anyone being diagnosed under the new, all-inclusive classification does not feel that this book does not apply to them.

The purpose of this book is to provide guidance to you, an individual with Asperger syndrome or ASD who is considering starting your own business, in order to assist you to become a confident and successful entrepreneur and professional of a business with your own culture and values – one in which you no longer struggle to fit in, but in which you set the example.

Part 5 contains a number of toolkits and exercises which are available to be downloaded from www.jkp.com/catalogue/book/9781849055093/resources.

PART 1

Understanding What it Takes to be an Entrepreneur

Chapter 1

Understanding Entrepreneurship and the Entrepreneur

What do we mean when we talk about becoming an entrepreneur? What exactly is an 'entrepreneur'? What in particular are we discussing when we talk about 'entrepreneurship' or 'entrepreneurial flair'?

Even if you feel you are familiar with the term 'entrepreneurship' and its definition, can I suggest that you still skim through this chapter, since I will also be discussing how the definition of entrepreneur and entrepreneurship applies to people with Asperger syndrome in particular, rather than purely providing an academic account.

Entrepreneur and entrepreneurship defined

When we start to talk about entrepreneurship and becoming an entrepreneur, many people feel quite confident about the definitions of these terms. In general, an entrepreneur is seen as someone who starts their own business, and entrepreneurship means the process of starting up your own business. While this definition is not strictly incorrect, it is certainly incomplete, and before you start thinking about making the move to becoming an entrepreneur, it is important that you understand what the term is actually describing.

Academically, there are two terms we need to review. The first of these is the term 'entrepreneur'. A number of business scholars over the years have worked to provide an appropriate definition of this term that adequately describes exactly what an entrepreneur is and does. Despite this being seen as a relatively new area by most people, the term 'entrepreneur' has been around for centuries. One of the first references I have been able to find has been by Richard Cantillon (1680s–1734), an Irish-French economist and author of *Essai sur la Nature du Commerce en Général* (Essay on the Nature of Trade in

General). He effectively divided society into two key classes: those who were fixed income wage-earners and those who were non-fixed income earners. Entrepreneurs, according to Cantillon, were non-fixed income earners who were willing to buy at a certain price but earn uncertain incomes, due to an unknown demand for their product (Cantillon 2001). Joseph Schumpeter (1935), on the other hand, emphasised the influence of entrepreneurs in his definition of them. He stated that the innovation and technological changes of a nation came from entrepreneurs, or wild spirits. Researchers such as Gartner (1988) and Aldrich and Wiedenmayer (1993) have defined an entrepreneur as a person who creates new, independent organisations that add value through a product or service.

It can be seen from these definitions that the core understanding of an entrepreneur is someone who does not have a fixed income, who is a risk-taker and who creates new businesses that add value through a product or a service. I believe the last element mentioned here, namely that the business should add value, is an important consideration, especially as we seek to set up our own businesses.

The second term we need to review is 'entrepreneurship'. This is slightly more expansive than 'entrepreneur' since it includes not only a description of the person but the activities undertaken by them as well.

By far the best definition for entrepreneurship I have read has been proposed by Shane and Venkataraman (2000, p.218), who state that entrepreneurship is '…a process that involves the discovery, evaluation and exploitation of opportunities to introduce new products, services, processes, ways of organising, or markets'.

Entrepreneurship involves more than just giving up a fixed income and starting a new company. This formal definition emphasises that the entrepreneurial process includes elements of creativity, insight and courage as the individual identifies an opportunity and proactively goes out to make it a successful reality. This definition leads in well to a discussion of what have been identified as the competencies and skills that potential entrepreneurs require in order to be successful.

An entrepreneur's competencies and motivation

A question we frequently hear asked in academic (and business) circles is whether entrepreneurs are born or made. Do efficacious entrepreneurs have an inborn ability to create and drive new business ideas, or have they been in an environment that has enabled them to learn the necessary skills to do this?

Is success as an entrepreneur the result of certain innate personality traits, meaning that people without those traits are likely to be ineffective?

These questions have been researched academically since the beginning of the twentieth century. I now provide a brief summary of the findings over the years to inform our review of our own potential for entrepreneurship.

Linking entrepreneurial success to personality traits of the entrepreneur

Research undertaken in the early twentieth century investigated the economic success of organisations relative to certain personality factors of the entrepreneurs who established them. Researchers such as Schumpeter (1935) and McClelland (1961) proposed that there was a link between economic growth and factors such as innovativeness, motivation, dominance and risk taking. After 1980, there was a very noticeable shift from associating the success of the new business largely with economic or societal factors, to that of associating success with the personality of the actual business owner.

A very successful model was developed by Rauch and Frese (2000) who identified six key personality traits possessed by effective entrepreneurs. I expand on these identified traits below.

Need for achievement

People who have a high need for achievement are those who tend to take personal responsibility for their performance at work, actively seek feedback on their performance from others, and are constantly searching for better and more effective ways of working. According to research, they tend to prefer moderately challenging tasks rather than routine or very difficult ones, since they know there is a high probability of their being successful in completing these tasks effectively. Additional research showed a positive correlation between an entrepreneur's need for achievement and business success (Rauch and Frese 2007; Collins, Hanges and Locke 2004). It is therefore recognised as a very important characteristic for potential entrepreneurs.

Innovativeness

Innovativeness refers to the entrepreneur's ability to introduce new products, services and ideas. It also assumes the individual's willingness and interest in looking for novel ways of working (Drucker 1985; Schumpeter 1935). Research has shown that innovativeness of the entrepreneur has a very positive relation to the success of the new business (Drucker 1985, pp.19–33). Examples of this can also be seen in the work undertaken by the Imperial College London Business School's department of Innovation and Entrepreneurship.

Autonomy

Individuals with a high need for autonomy are those who want to be in control of their lives and how they work, and who avoid the restrictions of what they see as the bureaucracy of the rules of established organisations (Brandstätter 1997). Most autonomous people long passionately to establish their own ways of thinking rather than conforming to the norm. Daniel Pink provides a number of excellent examples of how the introduction of autonomy into certain organisations has allowed creativity and entrepreneurial skills to grow (Pink 2010). However, it was also recognised that too high a need for autonomy was seen as a negative trait, since these individuals often struggled to cooperate with others.

Internal locus of control

An internal locus of control means that an individual believes in controlling their own destiny and future (Rotter 1996). People with a strong internal locus of control tend to start their business believing that the success or failure of the organisation is determined directly by them, rather than holding that this is a consequence of circumstances or the external environment. This personality trait tends to be very closely related to that of autonomy, and is understandably important in how much effort an entrepreneur puts into his or her company.

Self-efficacy

The psychologist Albert Bandura developed the concept of self-efficacy in the 1970s as part of his social cognitive theory. Bandura defined self-efficacy as 'the belief in one's capabilities to organize and execute the courses of action required to manage prospective situations' (1995, p.2). In other words, self-efficacy is a person's belief in his or her ability to succeed in a particular situation. Bandura described these beliefs as determinants of how people think, behave, and feel.

Risk taking

Chell, Haworth and Brearley (1991, p.42) described a risk taker as someone 'who in the context of a business venture, pursues a business idea when the probability of succeeding is low'. For people who are considering becoming entrepreneurs, therefore, it is likely that they have higher levels of risk taking tendencies, since entrepreneurship relates to making decisions under conditions of uncertainty. Therefore, individuals who are more risk tolerant are more likely to start a business than those who are more wary of taking risks (Knight 2006).

Of all the personality traits that have been identified to date, this last one may present those of us on the autism spectrum with the most significant challenge. Most people on the spectrum are generally not natural risk takers in the sense of stepping out of our comfort zones, or eagerly changing our established ways of thinking and working.

While these six personality traits are still recognised as important today, I would also add an additional four personality traits which I feel are equally – if not more – important for entrepreneurs. I believe that we, as people with ASD, often do well as entrepreneurs because we tend to have extremely strong tendencies towards these four personality traits, and any potential shortcoming in the area of risk taking is frequently overcome by these.

Dedication

One of the most important personal characteristics of an entrepreneur is that of dedication. Whether this is a person who is either going to make the transition from the corporate world into the entrepreneurial world, or take the bold step of starting up their own business straight after school or university, a potential entrepreneur needs to be dedicated not only to their business vision, but also to overcoming successfully any and all challenges they face in getting their business started, running and ultimately growing. Entrepreneurs need to be dedicated to their new company, to their new staff and to their new customers or stakeholders.

Persistence

Another important personality trait of an entrepreneur is the ability to make persistence an integral part of the way they work and think. Sometimes a potential entrepreneur can display all of the personality traits accepted as characteristic of successful entrepreneurs, and yet their ideas fail due to their inability to keep going when problems arise, timescales appear difficult or they face criticism or challenges. Persistence can be invaluable in ensuring that you actually achieve your goals without surrendering too easily with a cry of 'I give up – this must have been a bad idea.'

Passion

The personal characteristic of passion is beginning to be more acknowledged by business researchers and organisational psychologists as a trait that is linked to entrepreneurial success, although I am surprised that it hasn't always been so. Passion is what drives us to go the extra mile, to make those difficult choices, to 'stick our necks out' and just go for it. On its own, passion isn't going to determine whether or not a person will decide to become an entrepreneur. After all, there are many individuals who are extremely successful in their corporate careers directly as a result of the fact that they are passionate about what they do – in that environment. These people probably wouldn't be interested in an entrepreneurial career because their passion is in the corporate world. However, for those people who are passionate about an idea or vision that can be met through entrepreneurial means, passion is a key trait to driving the success of that vision.

Enthusiasm

One may think that enthusiasm is the same as – or even overshadowed by – passion. However, there is a distinction between these two personality traits that can make a big difference in how successful an entrepreneur can be. In general, passion is something that is internally focused. Although we frequently think of someone who is passionate as being someone we can visibly recognise as being so, this isn't actually a correct definition. A person who is passionate holds something very dear to his or her heart. If they feel passionately about something – a business vision, a relationship, a hobby – it is something that they will focus all their energies on, sometimes to the detriment of other areas of their lives. It is an internal commitment, a personal mindset, a feeling that cannot be denied within you. On the other hand, when we talk about seeing that someone is passionate, we are talking about something else. This can be seen in a statement made by someone I met at a conference once, who said to me, 'I can see you really are passionate about [this topic]. You really are so enthused, it's inspirational.' The perception of passion can be seen in the second sentence here – it is related to being enthused: in other words, enthusiastic. Enthusiasm is the outward expression of passion and without it your individual passion will be nowhere near as effective as it could in making you a successful entrepreneur.

An entrepreneur's enthusiasm has the effect of acting almost like a magnet, drawing people to them, their ideas and their businesses. People are drawn to the energy and excitement, often wanting to share in what they see being generated.

The dedication, persistence, passion and enthusiasm towards something we feel strongly about that people on the spectrum usually display can often take people by surprise. That said, however, it is really important to recognise that these same strengths can sometimes end up being potential shortcomings if we are not careful. This will become clearer as you work your way through the rest of the book.

Chapter 2

Why do People Decide to Become Entrepreneurs?

There are a multitude of reasons why people decide to go into business for themselves. Some of these generic reasons apply to those of us with Asperger syndrome or autism spectrum disorder (ASD) as much as they apply to any neurotypical. However, there are some additional reasons why many Asperger professionals decide to make the move to entrepreneurship that neurotypical individuals would not be able to understand or identify with.

For most of us on the spectrum, our careers are not just our jobs – what we do from day to day to earn a living and pay the mortgage or rent. We *are* our work. It tends to be a very integral part of who we are and is strongly linked to how we see ourselves. It defines us, it gives us a sense of self-worth and it reflects our values. For that reason, most of us will go to extraordinary lengths to become successful in a career we feel is reflective of us, but we can become extremely frustrated when we feel our ability to progress as we know we can in that area is hampered by things outside out control.

I have found that the decision processes for individuals wanting to go into their own businesses do have some differences depending on whether or not the person concerned is currently an Asperger professional in the corporate world or whether they have yet to reach the corporate career ladder at all. For this reason, I am going to discuss the process from two separate perspectives: first that of an individual who has yet to get started in the business world, such as a school-leaver or college graduate, and second that of the Asperger professional who is making the decision to become an entrepreneur after having had a successful career in the corporate world.

Becoming an entrepreneur as a first career

Finding a job as a person on the spectrum is often recognised as one of the more challenging things in our lives. This generally has nothing to do with our capabilities or potential, but is related to how the neurotypical world perceives us and our 'differences'. The corporate world places an inordinately high premium on teamwork and 'culture-fit', even in the type of jobs where we would not consider this so important. For those of us with Asperger's, this can create an issue. We leave school or college generally confident in our abilities to do our work and undertake a career in the area we have chosen. Our focus has been on performance of the particular type of work we are going to do in our new career, not on the 'fitting-in' element. In fact, the realisation that this is still expected of us beyond school and college can be very demotivating and demeaning as the point is drilled home that we are different, and that we will ultimately need to fit into 'their' world.

Some people with ASD make the decision to start their own businesses after having gone through a challenging experience in respect of finding work. In this case, starting your own business could feel like a far better option than losing confidence as a result of incessant interviews where your shortfalls are emphasised and your competence questioned purely because you are different. Ross, an entrepreneur from the United Kingdom, found this particularly challenging in his job search:

> I achieved excellent grades in my exams and I knew my stuff. I knew what I wanted to do – I just felt I needed to find the best company for me. I had – as was required with my qualification – undertaken some internship work within a large practice in London, and I know my work had been acknowledged as above standard and insightful, since I had received a copy of my feedback report from my lecturer. When I started to look for work, however, I found that it wasn't a case of me having a number of interviews and me picking the best fit at all. It turns out most of my applications were coming back as 'we regret's' before I even got invited to an interview. I was very frustrated by this and asked advice from my previous lecturer, since he was one of the few educators I had actually established a rapport with. He told me it was in all likelihood related to my feedback sheet for my internship, which needed to be submitted with my applications, because in this the evaluator had mentioned that although my levels of work were extremely good and I had potential, I was not a team player and tended to be a loner. It seems that this observation totally overshadowed the comments about the level of my work, and was [sic] all the recruiting companies were interested in, instead of what I could offer them as an individual. That's why I decided to start my own business – after eight months of not even getting one invitation to interview, you realise something isn't right.

Ross' experience is sadly not unique. While many people do not have a situation where they need to submit internship evaluations as part of their applications, teamworking and independence issues can arise in the interview process. In addition, some people are quite open about their ASD on their application forms, and this is not always a very prudent approach, since many employers are still very ignorant about what Asperger's or ASD really is and as a result they may automatically dismiss the candidate as having a 'performance cap'.

Fortunately, things have improved significantly over the last seven or eight years in respect of the workplace. Many companies have become less prescriptive in respect of things such as dress codes, workplace cultures, and hours. Laws introduced many years ago meant to ensure that we all have equal opportunities in the workplace and are not discriminated against are more genuinely adhered to, as opposed to being just compliance window-dressing. However, that said, in order to take advantage of that protection we must first have a job, and second have made a disclosure to our employer that we are on the autism spectrum, a decision one should not take lightly as I emphasise above.

Some ASD people have started their businesses straight from school due to being approached by a family member or friend who has suggested that this may be good for them. In some of these cases, the person who has recommended the entrepreneurial route to them has joined with them in the business, but sometimes they have just served as a support system for the individual outside their business.

A large number of people also make the decision to start their own businesses after having seen someone close to them do the same thing. Aaron, an entrepreneur from Australia, says: 'My father, a professor in Computer Science, founded an internet company in which I was briefly involved. This led me to found my own internet company.'

Simon, an entrepreneur from Australia, had a similar experience: 'The opportunity was presented to me so I took it. I come from a family of independent small/medium business owners and I liked the idea of not having to play the corporate game.'

Another reason why some people decide to make starting their own business their first career is because they have not had the opportunity to finish the required level of education in order to follow their desired career. This is highlighted well by Gwyneth, an entrepreneur from London. She shares:

> My interest is in a scientific field in which I have only informal training and self-taught knowledge, and no degrees. As a person without school qualifications the higher degrees I would need to do professional work in my field of interest seem virtually unattainable because of the extreme time and cost involved. As I have a need to get on with my chosen career now, self-employment seemed the only viable option. The corporate world will

not offer me anything better than secretarial work, which does not use my intellect and does not provide a way to follow my special interest.

Gwyneth's experience highlights another challenge that many people on the spectrum experience when looking for work, and that is that they are frequently faced with being offered jobs only for what we would call lower-level jobs, or those that do not make use of our intellects or our special interests. This challenge is also highlighted by Patrick (not real name), an entrepreneur from the south of England. 'Finding a job at the appropriate level was a nightmare,' he says. He continues:

> Despite the fact that I have a doctorate degree and am more than qualified to work as a practitioner, whenever I applied for practitioner roles I was unsuccessful. What I find incomprehensible is the fact that I wasn't even considered for Associate Practitioner roles – the only offers I received were for Office Junior and Assistant to the Associate Practitioner. Obviously, there was no way I could take this level of role, since most people who are Associate Practitioners don't even have a Masters in the field, let alone a doctorate. When I asked for feedback from a couple of them, they said they needed to have time to see if I could work at that level. I think I made a mistake telling them I had Asperger syndrome, but they asked the question on the application form about disability – I thought they needed to know.

Irrespective of the reasons why people decide to start their own businesses without going into the corporate environment, there can be no doubt that there are both significant pros and cons to a direct entry (if I can call it that) as opposed to a second career entry from a corporate environment. On the negative side, people who have never worked in the formal corporate world sometimes feel that they are at a disadvantage when it comes to the business world, not being familiar with business terminologies, practices and processes. Some people do not even realise that they have a shortcoming in this area – and to be frank, they are sometimes better off than those people who are aware of the shortcoming in their knowledge. Why do I say this? Well, this is because when we are aware of a gap in our knowledge, we tend to focus on that and either spend a lot of time and effort trying to fill the gap, or we are put off doing what we should be doing for fear of the potential of our making a mistake because of that lack of knowledge and experience. As such, we can become paralysed as far as moving forward with a new business is concerned, instead focusing on trying to fill a perceived gap. In reality, the fact that you do not have corporate 'habits' can actually be a great positive for you in starting your own business because, as I will highlight in Part 2 of this book, the way in which people operate within a corporate setting is very different from the way people operate within a small business.

There certainly are things that you would be wise to find out about as your start your entrepreneurial career if you have no other knowledge of the business world. This book will assist you in finding that information, as well as reassuring you that the level of knowledge you actually require for this is potentially not quite as extensive as you imagined.

Becoming an entrepreneur after a corporate career

There are many Asperger professionals who make the decision to enter the entrepreneurial world after many years in a successful corporate career. There can be a number of reasons for this. One of the most obvious of these is the desire many of us have to work and be successful in an environment where we are not constantly struggling to fit in – to excel in an environment free from people-related constraints. Almost without exception, those of us with ASD working in the corporate world are *always* having to focus on making sure we fit in, always working to ensure we do things the neurotypical way, always putting in that extra effort to ensure we have not made a slip in any of the areas we find challenging. The appeal of working in an environment where we do not have to make *fitting in* the centre of our work experience can be inspirational.

Without a doubt, the most common element of that challenge relates to office politics – the proverbial ASD nightmare in the workplace. Allison Bruning, CEO/Founder of Mountain Springs House talks of her experience of the challenges of the corporate world:

> My greatest challenge in the education world was not understand [sic] the social games people play. I have never been able to hold onto a job for very long. I never lost my job because my boss was dissatisfied with my work. On the contrary, my bosses have always told me I am a hard worker and they appreciate everything I have done. The reason I lose my jobs is because I wouldn't understand the social cues my co-workers gave nor the games they would play. Things would get stressful in the workplace and I would lose my job.

In a similar vein, entrepreneur Simon adds:

> ...inability to play politics – taking things personally all the time (I've become much better at that, though) – managing situations with difficult people – fitting in – I just wasn't interested in their small talk and had to force myself to get involved in others conversations so I could feel that I belong. Social situations – always felt uncomfortable in work social scenarios and would always try to avoid them.

'Factoring political agendas into how to deal with senior executives was a challenge,' shares Stewart, an entrepreneur from the UK. 'I instinctively just tell "the truth"… Respecting individuals who were senior, but who "talked rubbish" (at least in my perception) was a challenge. Even if I could restrain myself from criticising them in public it was difficult for my views not to be obvious to everyone… Reading social signals and body language became a problem and I was prone to saying the wrong thing at the wrong time.'

Gwyneth's experience of the corporate world highlights the social challenges:

> The corporate world values number of years on a similar type of job and 'fitting the culture' over one's actual knowledge and skills, and expects staff – particularly support staff – to fit a very narrow range of personality characteristics which I feel that I cannot meet and am no longer willing to pretend. I am the archetypical absent-minded professor, but had to work in offices to pay the bills. In my last job they tried to frame my quiet personality and intellectual interests as passivity and lack of social skills, and it was when they tried to get me on 'performance' grounds that I sought diagnosis. The performance criteria were highly subjective: items like 'team player', 'attitude' and 'initiative' that could have been interpreted as many different ways as there were people writing up the assessment. My detailed subject knowledge, strong technical skills, and speed/accuracy of work were all downplayed, while every trivial error and minor disagreement during the working day were reported to HR. I felt bullied and ostracized. The ridiculous thing is that I could easily have done any of their jobs had I had the same opportunities to go to school. I have an extremely high IQ (>4SD) but without the formal schooling that one would need to occupy a career that would make use of it (e.g. scientific research and academia), even though those are my true interests in life. Put an Aspie who is a frustrated scientist in an admin support role and it's probably a recipe for misunderstandings and/or resentments by bosses and colleagues. Those type of pay-the-bills jobs were, unfortunately, all my formal qualifications and work experience could get me.

Many people will identify with the examples given above, but there are some individuals who have been fortunate enough to work in corporate environments where this has not created a problem, even if there was an awareness of the issue. Scott Sheinfeld, Founder of Infected Sloths LLC observes:

> Well, I really didn't know what it all meant, so at the time, I just accepted I was different. But in retrospect, I was obviously an outsider socially. Really never participated in rumor mills, in fact was completely oblivious to those kind of things. I was always looked at as 'different' or 'a little odd', but that was ok by me…and by them eventually. After people came to know what I did, they would always say 'it's ok, he's creative' and I'd take that as a compliment.

Additional reasons for making the move into an entrepreneurial career can be related to the actual work environment and the effectives of such things as hypersensitivities of people with Asperger's or ASD. Stewart explains: 'Sensory overload became an issue as I was running a major transformation programme with Group Sponsors and stakeholders in USA and suppliers in India. Emails and phone calls were incessant. At the time I was not aware enough (pre-diagnosis) of what was going on to manage this effectively.' Similarly James, an entrepreneur from east coast USA, notes 'My greatest challenge was around the workplace itself. I have sensitivities to loud noises and the overhead lights in the office. When things get busy, I can start to go into overload because my senses can't seem to cope. But in the corporate world there is nothing you can do – you can't just walk out or find a breakaway area. Sometimes you can't even lock yourself in the [toilet] for long enough without someone looking for you.'

'I dislike air conditioning and artificial lights,' says Gwyneth. She goes on:

I would rather sit by a window that I can open. Sensitive to noise and motion. I have an auditory discrimination problem that makes it hard to hear phone calls and conversations in a noisy environment. The worst thing is I hate people walking or standing behind my chair, approaching me from behind, or seeing my screen/watching me type. In my last job I had been seated literally backing onto the intersection of two corridors with the foot traffic of two departments stamping up and down all day. HR only finally heeded my many requests for a change of desk location after formal diagnosis and a recommendation from the Occupational Health doctor.

Stewart highlights a very common challenge that people on the spectrum face in working within the corporate environment today, and that is the open plan office. This is echoed by Ross, who shares: 'I cannot understand the appeal of the open plan office. Ok, financially I get it. But it is like trying to work in a railway station most of the time. People are loud, inconsiderate and – sometimes – even smelly! They stomp around creating visual and proximity issues for me, and I struggle to focus and end up snapping at people.'

Denise, an entrepreneur from South Africa, says:

The trouble with the open plan is that there is just too much distraction for me. I hear everything people say because I have overly strong hearing and can't block things out like normal [sic] people can. I find the only way I can work is to focus so deeply on what I am doing that I become oblivious to everything around me – I blank it out, the same way I blanked everything out when I was a child. The trouble is, people will then come and talk to me and I will not hear them because I am in my own blanked out world of focus, then people think I am ignoring them. It causes a lot of problems.

Another key reason why many people decide to move is due to miscommunication and a lack of shared understanding of the value of the work being done. Aaron, an entrepreneur from Australia, provides a good example of this:

> I was required to deliver mundane tasks that very few others would have been interested [sic]. I would love to tell you working like this was richly rewarding, but the truth is it wasn't! While speedily completing the work at first, surprisingly it was easy to become sidetracked when I finally identified more rewarding tasks for me. Unknown to me, I had miscalculated these would align with the company's own objectives. I was sternly confronted by [my boss], resulting in a few staff members quickly excusing themselves from our presence. I never regained the same focus I had initially and was pleased when the time came to part ways. Clearly this would have been due to poor communications and lack of recognition in me wanting to play a more critical role!

After discussing all the negative reasons for people wanting to make a move from the corporate world to the entrepreneurial, we should end with a look at some of the more positive reasons why people decide to move.

A number of people – both those on the spectrum and neurotypicals – make the move because they identify a gap or shortfall in the marketplace that they have the skills, knowledge or resources to address. Often, those of us on the spectrum can identify areas that we are very passionate about, specifically things like addressing perceived injustices or inequities.

Allison Bruning shares: 'I had worked as an educator and an author before I started my publishing house. I was very frustrated with how hard it was for authors to publish their works. I wanted to combine my educational and literary career into a business where I could help other authors navigate through the publishing world and achieve their literary dreams.'

Jeremy Samson, Founder and Managing Director of Time2Train tells us: 'I was working in the gym and was approached by a family that wanted to their son to improve his fitness, as he had aspergers, so I had a bright idea to simply give back to the community especially in the field of autism/aspergers by creating a training program to help others that shared the same condition as myself – Asperger syndrome."

Whatever the motivation for taking the decision to leave the corporate world to start an entrepreneurial career, it is important for the person making the move to recognise *all* their underlying motivations for making the move. Why is this important, you may ask? Well, often people will decide to start their businesses to fulfil a personal goal or to overcome a challenge, and they will focus on this as the key measurement of their success. However, down the line, they may find that they are starting to feel disappointed in their business for some reason, even if it is successful as a business. Patrick (not real name) provides a good example of this.

Case study: Patrick's software business

Patrick had been working as a software engineer in a medium-sized corporation for many years and had played a role in developing some very successful software programmes over a number of years. Over the last few years, Patrick had become frustrated that his employers were not listening to him when he advised them that the world of corporate software was changing and that more and more corporations were looking for cloud-based solutions. He knew what he was talking about, and he even offered potential solutions to his employers, but they appeared to be set in their ways and blind to the changes occurring around them. As an employee, he had no say in the direction the company was taking, and this annoyed him almost as much as seeing the wasted opportunities.

Eventually, Patrick took the decision to resign from his job and start his own small business, developing cloud-based software solutions. He had the skills necessary to develop the solutions and he loved his work – what could go wrong?

Patrick started his business with money he had put away over the years. It didn't require too much of an investment in the beginning, and it was only later that he realised he would need to have some kind of office presence for potential clients if he was to be credible in their eyes – virtual offices were just not cutting it.

Eventually Patrick and his small team of programmers developed a solution he knew would meet the needs of his target audience, the medium-sized corporation. He started his sales calls and subsequent client meetings as soon as he had a demonstration product, and within a short time he had a number of clients signed up. However, as part of getting these clients to take a chance on a new company and a new product, they had insisted that their contact with his company be with him personally, since he had a good reputation in the marketplace. As a consequence, Patrick inadvertently became account manager for the first ten clients they signed up.

While the success of his business was certainly incredibly motivating for Patrick, he started to struggle to find the motivation to get to the business every day. Whereas previously he tended to wake with the birds and be the first person in the office and the last to leave, now it was a challenge to even get out of bed in the morning, and he started arriving at the office later and later. Eventually he began to miss client meetings, much to their frustration, and things reached a head when two of his clients terminated their contracts.

Patrick was overwhelmed and confused. What was happening to him? He had the independence he wanted, the financial resources he needed, the control he craved and the reality of a vision that could have been lost if he had not created it himself. Why wasn't he ecstatic as he should be?

Patrick's example highlights a situation that unfortunately does occur in a number of cases. As Patrick asked himself in the end, why was it that he was not happy with his situation? Surely it was everything he had wanted. In meeting with Patrick and discussing his situation, it became apparent that there were potentially two main reasons why he was struggling to enjoy his new company. In the first instance, Patrick had ended up taking on a lot more client interaction as part of his role than he thought he would. He had never intended to be an account manager at all. As a result, he felt that his time was no longer under his own control anymore as it had been when he first started his business. His demanding clients were controlling his time, and this made him feel more like an employee than a business owner. Second, his passion was for coding, not business development, sales or account management. Yet he had ended up being the key account manager for his company, and he had no time to do any coding at all. His passion had been passed down to his programming team, and he felt himself yearning to be in their place instead of his own. *They* were living the dream, not him. He had, in fact, created a company that addressed his needs as he perceived them, not as they actually were.

To make sure that you do not run the risk of starting up your own business only to be frustrated down the line, I would recommend you spend a few minutes completing the Toolkit Exercise 1 in Part 5 of the book. Once you have completed that, return to your reading in this chapter.

An important consideration for people leaving the corporate world to become an entrepreneur is that there are differences in the way a person in an entrepreneurial environment will need to work compared to how people tend to work within a corporate one. This ties to Part 2 of this book that addresses those people who are specifically moving from a corporate career to an entrepreneurial one. You may find this part of the book useful in ensuring that the way you operate going forward is optimal for the sort of career you have now moved into. Even if you are not moving from a corporate career but starting your business as a first career, I recommend that you at least skim through this section, since it may reassure you that some areas that you thought important to know about and be able to do may not actually be so critical in a small business.

PART 2

Moving from a Corporate Job to an Entrepreneurial Career

Chapter 3

Strategic Planning and Decision Making as an Entrepreneur

For those people on the autism spectrum who have been able to develop a successful career within the corporate world, making the move to owning their own business may feel less of a challenge than it may be for others who have not had the benefit of many years of business management and leadership experience. Frequently, we make the decision to leave the corporate world once we have reached the pinnacle of our career within that world. Surely, then, those years have given us invaluable insights and experience that can transfer across directly to a small business?

In all honesty, however, the habits and experiences we have internalised within our corporate employment environment can often end up being detrimental to the start-up of a small business, without the entrepreneur even realising it. This can be especially true for those of us on the autism spectrum, as we tend to avoid changing ways of working that have been successful for us in the past. For many a senior executive this may seem counter-intuitive. After all, the skills that they have developed over the years are exactly what made them such successful professionals within the corporate world. A small business started by an entrepreneur is still a business – shouldn't the same principles apply? Well, in many instances the answer is – no!

As any successful business professional within the corporate world will tell you, a large part of a business leader's role is focused on strategic planning, formal structures and established rules. In the corporate world we do a lot of formal business planning and reporting – it is essential for the on-going development and operation of a corporate entity. In the entrepreneurial world, however, we need to think differently and start to condense the process.

Decision making in general

Within the corporate world, decisions taken by professionals need to be closely tied to short-term, medium-term and long-term strategic plans. As a result, managers and professionals ensure that strategic decisions are taken only after appropriate meetings, liaison with stakeholders and alignment to the corporate strategy has taken place. This often means that key decisions require a number of meetings or a formal approval processes before they can be actioned.

In becoming an entrepreneur, one of the areas where you will find a difference in your decision-making process is that decisions are far more short-term and immediate that those you would have taken responsibility for as a senior professional in the corporate world. In fact, it would be more accurate to say that decisions taken as an entrepreneur are more temporary than they are in the corporate world. Let me clarify what I mean with another case study.

Case study: Philip S. and his website design company

Philip S. was a highly successful IT Director within a large multinational company head-quartered in Reading, UK. Despite his success and specialist reputation in the corporate world, Philip never really enjoyed his job. It wasn't that he didn't enjoy the highly specialised, technical part of the work – in fact, he was well-known in the corporate world due to his knowledge, experience and skill – but since he had become a leader with his company, the majority of his job now focused on people management, strategic planning, budgeting and meetings. Philip felt this was related to his Asperger syndrome, which he had been diagnosed with in his late twenties.

One day, Philip attended an IT conference in London, something he usually did not do that often, since he generally found the crowds and noise stressful. However, his CEO had mentioned to him that he felt it was important for the company to become more high profile at these conferences and – as the corporate IT Director – this was his responsibility.

Struggling to maintain his composure while experiencing high discomfort levels during the conference, Philip took the opportunity to stand outside the main conference room halfway through the conference, where it was far quieter. Wandering down the corridor, he half-heartedly read the posters on the walls advertising various services and software.

As he was about to stop and turn back, one poster caught his eye. It was for a web design company offering bespoke web and other graphic design work. Philip read it slowly, feeling a strange sense of excitement as he continued to do so. Yes! This was it! He had the skills. He had the technical knowledge. He had the contacts – and he had enough funds to invest in a company of his own. Philip resigned from his job the following month and after completing his six month notice period, he started his own company. As part of this, he recruited a team of ten young web designers and general IT advisors, as well as a staff manager, a business development manager, a finance manager and a general manager to deal with operations.

Philip was confident in his ability to establish his own company, and therefore did not seek any professional advice. He took a long time establishing a formal strategic plan for the company and related budgets, processes and authorisation rules. In terms of this, all decisions in respect of clients, expenditure and project work would go through appropriate decision-making channels, which consisted of initial business case meetings followed by relevant committee approval. In addition, there were monthly executive committee meetings (attended by himself, his finance manager and his general manager), budget meetings, business development meetings and strategic planning meetings.

Initially, this system appeared to be working well. Philip was familiar with the standard procedures, meetings and activities related to the running of his new business and his reputation saw their acquisition of a large number of clients. Philip was also very focused on new business development, since he knew that within the corporate world, the key indicator of success was sales and related revenue. He set sales targets for everyone in the business, and linked a small commission based incentive to the achievement of those targets.

However, as his client base began to grow, Philip noticed that timescales for completing work were beginning to slip. He also noticed that the team of people he had hired who were initially so enthusiastic and excited were beginning to turn up late for work, take long lunches and leave work at 5 p.m. on the dot. Philip struggled to understand where their enthusiasm had gone.

Philip also found that he was being challenged by his clients to come back with new ideas far quicker than he had planned, this resulting in his scheduled authorisation processes being challenged and sometimes skipped. This annoyed Philip, and he insisted that the processes that he had established in his business be meticulously followed – he knew what he was doing after all, having worked in the field for several years.

In some of the meetings that were held with the executive team, as he called them, concerns were raised by Dave, the business development manager, that there was a significant increase in the number of companies offering self-service website design. This was, he insisted, a significant risk for them, since they were charging reasonably high rates to a large number of small business clients, and it was feasible that within a short time they could make the decision to start designing and managing their own websites. Dave recommended that they start to develop their own 'self-service' offering, or at least look at some type of tie-in clause being added to the standard web design contracts.

Philip recognised that this was potentially important, but felt that this would go against this plans established earlier in the year in respect of product and service development. He insisted that if this type of change was going to be made, this was formally presented to the appropriate committees followed by a board meeting, and that any agreed changes follow the usual annual business review process. Dave argued that there was no time for this – current clients were already asking about the company's ability to offer these services. Philip – annoyed at being challenged – told Dave to comply with the procedures of the company and not be a 'hot-head'.

Things began to reach a crisis point when a few of his clients began to express their dissatisfaction with the company's services, ultimately deciding to develop their own websites, and a number of his team started to resign, including the business development manager, Dave.

The above case study reflects some of the traps that people leaving the corporate environment can fall into, and this is particularly true for people on the spectrum leaving corporate employment, because we tend to have a proclivity to avoid changing things that have worked for us in the past. Let's examine the case study in a bit more detail to determine some of these pitfalls.

Formal decision-making structures

Philip's instinctual approach to setting up his company was to replicate the formal structure and procedures he was so used to working with in his corporate job. Unfortunately, by setting up such a formal decision-making structure Philip had unintentionally created a relatively static business that was unable to keep up with the rapid changes that were occuring in his sector. The reality of small business is that many of the decisions which need to be taken for that business to be successful need to be made within a fraction of the time that would be acceptable within a corporate setting, and as a consequence authorisation processes which require committees and other lengthy formal structures just do not provide an appropriate operating model.

The best model for start-ups and small businesses is one where there is a much reduced planning period, covering a maximum of six months, as opposed to the long-term strategic and mid-term operational plans you would have been used to working around in your corporate job, where the focus is a minimum of one year. It is, of course, important that you have a longer-term vision for your company, but the difference is that it is just that – a vision, not a formal plan against which you plan your short-term activities. Having a shorter-term planning period allows the start-up or small business to be lean and flexible, able to make decisions in a much shorter timeframe, and thereby adapt more quickly to any situation. I will discuss this approach in more detail later in the book when I describe what is called adaptive planning. Suffice to say that the process of adaptive planning involves making a large number of small decisions rather than fewer, large and long-term ones.

Formal policies and procedures

Another problem that Philip inadvertently created was a situation of tension among his staff. This will be covered in more detail in Chapter 14, but we can clarify at this point that the challenge Philip's staff experienced was that they had made the decision to move into a start-up, in all likelihood for similar reasons as Philip, and yet they were being forced to operate in the same way they had with their corporate employer due to the extensive policies and procedures he introduced. It is highly likely that they had taken lower salaries and/or sacrificed corporate employee benefits in order to have some small business freedoms. Instead, they probably felt that they had done more of a lateral transfer to another corporate in respect of working style, with reduced financial rewards. As an entrepreneur on the autism spectrum, it is important for you to recognise that while policies, procedures and set ways of working may provide security and comfort to us, to other people they can be seen as bureaucratic and restrictive. Most people with high-functioning autism will acknowledge that while procedures and set ways of working that we have developed or had a hand in developing are useful and valuable for us, those that do not suit the way our minds process information or the way we think can be highly distressing and challenging for us.

If you are setting up your own business, I would strongly recommend that you think twice about being overly prescriptive in terms of formal policies and procedures. I do feel that there are certain processes that need to be agreed and formalised so that there is no confusion about how things get done (for example, who is responsible for signing off expenses, how often should clients be contacted, etc.), but in developing these, I suggest that you complete Toolkit Exercise 2 in Part 5 of the book.

Growth is not always a critical factor for success

Another area that is important to recognise from the case study is related to growth. As a corporate executive, we are completely focused on increase in sales or customer numbers as an indicator of success. Growth tends to be seen as a critical success factor in most companies, unless they already have a significant portion of the market, in which case the focus turns to retention of customer numbers. Consider now an observation that frequently comes as a surprise to many corporate executives moving into their own businesses.

Within an entrepreneurial business, there should never be the same focus on sales as there is within a corporate business.

'What?!' you may declare. Surely that cannot be true. As a start-up one of the most important things you need is new business in order to earn revenue! Surely that is an illogical statement.

Well, in fact it isn't, and let me explain why. First of all, as part of your planning for your business, you will be moving from your longer-term plans to more realistic, short-term adaptive plans. As part of this, you will be identifying how much new business you need to see you through in the next six months. However, your focus is not just going to be on sales. As an independent business, you will be competing with larger businesses for clients. You will need to have some very valuable USPs (unique selling points) in order to get clients to put their trust in your business as a start-up as opposed to the more established organisations they are used to working with. These USPs are frequently related to such things as customer service, more one-to-one contact with the client, a dedicated team for the client (since there is only one point of contact within your company) or a product of exceptional quality.

It is these USPs that you should be focusing on, not on sales. Yes, of course you will need to win business, but you will never retain clients if your customer service, product or contacts are not what you have promised.

Second, when you have sufficient clients in order for you to meet your budgets and targets for your planning period (which should be a dynamic six month period), you need to stop actively selling. I am not saying you should refuse to sell your product or take on a client if they approach you. What I am saying is that you need to stop *actively* selling. Stop going out and trying to win extra contracts or clients, or sell huge amounts products. Why? Because if you don't, your value added elements are going to suffer. If you are offering a service, you will start to offer less and less time to your existing clients in order that you can spend time with new ones, or if you are selling something you produce, standards could drop and faults or errors appear in the end product, or shipping deadlines could start to be missed due to too much needing to be done in a short timescale.

In short – small business is not always about *growth*. It is more about *value*. For many people leaving the corporate world, this can be a significant change in their mind-set. If you are someone on the spectrum who has spent their entire career to date working in an environment with a growth focus and way of working, this can be even more difficult to change – because it is a formal change in your thinking and way of working.

Flatter organisational structures

There is another element of successful entrepreneurship that can be explored following the above case study, and this is the subject of organisational structure. What created a problem for Philip in the above study was the way that he insisted on creating a formal corporate reporting structure for his staff. You will read more about this topic in Chapter 14 on building relationships in the workplace, but suffice to say here that he ended up alienating his key staff by introducing (or trying to introduce!) a corporate culture into a start-up. These two do not generally go well together. The culture needed within a start-up is very different to that required within a corporate setting. Trying to apply corporate culture will have the effect of stifling creativity and frustrating your most valuable people.

Start-up businesses need to have far flatter organisational structures compared to corporates – even small corporates. What this means is that there are fewer layers of people in between you and your front-line staff. In most cases, there may be only one layer between you and all your staff, and sometimes all staff will report directly to you. I am not going to discuss the dynamics of people structures here, because I cover it in Chapter 14, but it is an important consideration to keep in mind in setting up your systems or processes. You don't want to create the sort of 'he reports to him, who reports to her, who reports to him, etc.' structure you often see in bigger companies. Teamwork is a much more important concept. As a person who has an ASD, this can sometimes be seen as very challenging, but I hope to provide you with some guidance in respect of this in both the next chapter and Chapter 18 which will help you to cope with this more confidently.

For strategic planning and decision-making processes within an entrepreneurial environment, it is essential to understand that these do not disappear in the small business, but they do change. You will still need to plan, have a business model and think about your financial planning, but in a totally different way. Simon, an entrepreneur from Australia, made the following observation in speaking about the differences in working style in a small business: '…the hardest part was the fact that I usually only focus on one thing at a time. I couldn't think both strategically and tactically at the same time. And looking back, I wish I spent more time thinking strategically – i.e. [sic] I should have worked "on" the business, not "in" the business.' Simon's thoughts about his business reflect the importance of recognising that strategic planning is still important, even though the format has changed. Running a small business or start-up cannot just be day-to-day operations, or you will become stuck where you are without any idea of how to move forward. As you continue through the book, I will explain some more of the differences between corporate and entrepreneurial strategy, as well as providing tools to help you where challenges may exist.

Chapter 4

Differences in Entrepreneurial Operational Processes in General

You have seen in the previous chapter that people leaving the corporate world to move into the entrepreneurial environment need to make quite a significant change in their mind-sets when it comes to strategic planning and decision making. The same can also be said of many of the operational processes within a small business or start-up, but in general this does not really come as a surprise to most people.

As people on the autism spectrum, however, we do run slightly more of a risk of missing out on areas where there are changes to be made in the way we operate, particularly in those areas that relate to people. Therefore, I am going to spend some time talking about these changes, and will follow this up with some more general areas of change that you should ensure that you are familiar and comfortable with.

Entrepreneurship is more hands-on

One element of entrepreneurship that differs from the corporate environment is that your work is going to become a lot more hands-on. Many of us feel that this is not really a concern, and that we have largely been very hands-on in our roles as it is. However, I would challenge you to think a little more about that assumption.

When we talk about being more hands-on, most people tend to think about such things as not being able to delegate as much as they have in the past, having to do more of things like writing up reports and speaking directly to customers. For those of us on the spectrum, some of these elements can be challenging, but we know that it is something we will have to do. However, being more hands-on also includes some far more basic stuff, especially when you are a start-up. Think about your work in the corporate world. You have a meeting with a client for a potential new piece of work. What do you do to prepare? Well, in most cases this would include asking your assistant or PA to get the file out for the client, and possibly do some research on the topic in question. You would ask her or him to schedule your travel to the client's office and advise the appropriate member of the sales team to accompany you. You would arrange for someone to take minutes in the meeting, and afterwards you would have these transcribed, sent through to all parties and filed. I am sure you will think of some additional actions you would take as well.

In a start-up company, in all likelihood you would be undertaking most of these activities yourself – including things you may never have had to do before, like filing, booking travel, taking notes in a meeting, drawing up contracts and so on. This was very well summarised by Scott Sheinfeld, founder of Infected Sloths LLC who, when asked about challenges he experienced in working as an entrepreneur that he did not realise were related to his ASD, said: 'The little things about running a business that seem to slip through my focus. I want to run my business using my knowledge in a specific field and bring that knowledge to other businesses in my own brand. Payroll? Accounts receivable? Purchasing supplies? Sure I know they are all VERY important, but day-to-day operations, whereas my focus is with my customers. I need to be reminded that there are other things that need to be done.'

Now, it is not to say that you definitely have to do all these things yourself. If you have sufficient funds, you may make the decision to hire an assistant to help you. In some respects that can be very useful, especially if you are the type of person with high-functioning autism who can get distracted by too much detail and by getting things 'ordered and orderly'. It is very easy to fall into the trap of developing a complex (albeit very functional) filing system rather than getting on with the focal work within your business, or taking times ensuring that a document is formatted and presented in the best possible way as opposed to hurrying up and getting it to the client to sign.

Many of the people on the spectrum who are entrepreneurs that I have spoken with have indicated that an area they consider both a great strength but also potentially a challenge is that of intense focus. Asking them about what they considered to be advantages their ASD gave them in the corporate environment, Aaron, an Australian entrepreneur, made the following comment: 'My unique ability to be singly focused assisted me [sic] deliver the mundane tasks assigned where few others would have been interested.' Allison Bruning, CEO/Founder of Mountain Springs House notes: 'My greatest advantage had to be my work ethic. I'm a go-getter and task oriented. My Asperger's has allowed me the opportunity to focus on a task until completion. I love to research and I would dig deep to get to the bottom of a problem in order to solve it. I also live a life of routine. My day has to be strictly scheduled which means I do well with a structured work environment.' Simon, another Australian entrepreneur, added: '…ability to focus, when I had to, on tasks. Hated solutions that were not perfect (often to my detriment because sometimes the job just has to be good enough, not perfect).' Similarly Scott Sheinfeld says: 'I also had the advantage of extreme focus. They knew if I was put in charge of a project, I would obsessively concentrate on it till it was complete.' Stewart Rapley, an entrepreneur from the UK also acknowledges that focus was a key Asperger strength in the corporate world: 'Focus and intensity,' he said, 'I was able to "hold course" despite the various things that seek to blow one off course the corporate context.'

There is no doubt after reading the above observations that focus is acknowledged as a key strength for people on the spectrum in the corporate world. However, as mentioned, this may potentially create a challenge for you in the entrepreneurial environment, where you do not have the time to focus on detail to the same extent that you were able in the corporate world. Many of us struggle with doing something less than 100 per cent, and leap at the opportunity to work for ourselves where we can ensure that everything is 100 per cent. But the reality of small business is that we often do not actually have the time to do that, since doing so will be to the detriment of other – often more important – activities.

Be aware at this time of any shortfalls you may have when it comes to things that are considered hands-on. Make sure that you put in back-up systems of your own to ensure you don't fall into traps. For example, I am just such a person who can get highly caught up in ensuring systems are organised and properly ordered. To ensure I avoid making that a focus, whenever I have to do anything to do with filing or organising, I set a timer on my computer which allows me only a certain amount of minutes before I am reminded that my allocated 'organising time' is almost over. I then have another ten minutes to finish my task before a final alarm advises me to stop the activity. I have found this extremely useful, but systems such as this will only be as useful as the attention you pay to them, and if you are actually aware of your challenge in the first place.

Changes relating to people

When we start our own businesses, there are three main categories of people we will be dealing with whom we need to consider; namely, employees and other stakeholders in your business, customers and suppliers. Is there a difference in the way we deal with them as an entrepreneur versus a corporate employee? Let us consider the three categories of people separately.

Employees
BROADER SPAN OF CONTROL

When you are working in a corporate environment, the nature of the organisation dictates that there tends to be quite a distance between you and your front-line staff. Communication with them almost always goes through at least one other level of people, such as department heads, senior managers, managers, team leaders and supervisors, dependent on your role within the company. In larger organisations, many leaders never even get to meet their front-line staff.

Working within an entrepreneurial environment is a completely different world. In order for a start-up or small business to operate effectively, many of these layers will never exist, and frequently all staff will actually report to you directly. As a result your operational span of control will significantly broaden from what you are accustomed to, if not your span of control in respect of headcount. What do I mean by this? Whereas as a leader of a particular part of the business or functional area you will tend to have a reporting structure made up of people in your area of expertise or focus, when you are running a small business or start-up, the people reporting to you will be from all areas of the business – technical, professional, administrative, operational. Therefore you will need to learn to communicate with different types of people. I know from personal experience, for example, that personalities and mind-sets of people generally working in areas like marketing or human resources are very different from those working in finance or IT. If you have worked in a corporate environment where you have only really had to deal with finance people, you may find it challenging to deal with the very lively and sociable characters who tend to work in marketing, for example. Be prepared for dealing with different types of people.

NO 'MANAGEMENT VERSUS WORKER'

Moving to an entrepreneurial environment means that you are moving away from a situation of formal management structures (or you should be!). As such, you are working on a far more level footing with your team than you would be in a corporate world. Despite the fact that employees are still employees, the reality is that due to the structure of a start-up or small business, the 'us versus them' mentality of management needs to be eradicated. You are all part of the same team now, and even if they ultimately report to you, they are working *with* you rather than reporting *in to* you.

Now, do not misunderstand what I am saying here. I am not saying that in an entrepreneurial environment everyone should all be 'pally-pally' and have no boundaries. Not at all. But what I am saying is that people tend to join small businesses because they long to have more independence, autonomy and freedom to make a difference in the company. If they join only to find that they really do not have those opportunities, it is unlikely they will stay for long. It is much more important to treat everyone equally in a small business than it is within the corporate world, because the roles people hold are all important for the business. If your receptionist goes off sick you usually do not have spare people to stand in for her or him, and getting in a temporary staff member can be time consuming and frankly too expensive.

It is important that you are more personable in a smaller business environment than formal. People need to identify with you, and this can be difficult to do if you are seen as distant and unapproachable. Often those of us with an autism spectrum disorder experience challenges when it comes to working so closely with people, and recognising their needs as far as their careers and how they work are concerned. One of the entrepreneurs interviewed (whom I have chosen to keep anonymous for this quotation) shared their concern in this area: 'I had [an employee] who left our company and threatened to sue [us]. I had no idea she was upset with me. We had chatted several times and never had appeared to be upset. Then out of the blue she told [sic] that I was cold-hearted and that I would never listen to her. I realised my Asperger's may have caused the communication problem between us. I tried to remedy the situation but it only made matters worse.' Although every situation is different, it is quite possible that the situation this Asperger professional experienced was as a direct result of working with someone who was expecting to have more of an input within a smaller business, and who would not have felt so strongly had this occurred in a corporate environment.

HIRING WHEN YOU NEED THEM – NOT IN CASE
Another area that needs to change as far as the topic of employees is concerned is that of recruitment.

As a business owner or entrepreneur coming from the corporate world, we can sometimes make the mistake of trying to resource our business to handle operations as they would be once the company was operating at optimal levels. Therefore, you could end up hiring a number of technical people, managers and admin staff, ahead of actually having the contracts that would provide them with work.

Within a start-up, it is important to hire people only as you need them. Start with the minimum number of staff you need to operate effectively in your type of business. As you win the contracts, you can then expand and grow. You do not need people sitting on the payroll draining your resources who do not actually have work to do.

What is important here is to make an accurate assessment of what staff are needed for you to start-up, and to be able to undertake your first contract. People may be concerned about this approach, saying that this could leave them in a difficult situation if they then win business and they do not already have the staff on-board to do the work. I do not agree with this outlook, although I do understand the concern. There are certain roles that can be difficult to recruit for, but these can still be formally recruited at the appropriate time without detriment to the business by following some suggestions:

- Hire enough staff to comfortably handle the work where you are now. If you have some additional work come in, there should be enough flexibility within the team to be able to take on some extra work until such time as additional resources are brought in.

- For difficult to recruit or key roles, work with a recruitment agency. Give an indication of when you think your role will become available, and ask them to do the necessary headhunting beforehand. These agencies are very good at maintaining interest in positions from candidates, and ensuring that there are always people down the pipeline.

- If you have specific people in mind who you are targeting, discuss with them the situation, and invite them to consider the option of either making themselves available to you in the near future when contracts come in, or to join the business bringing some business with them (hence ensuring new business).

Another area that I feel still falls under the topic of recruitment refers to the type of people you will be recruiting. As a professional, you will have brought people into your business who were either tactical, hands-on people at the operational side of the business, or strategic managers who have a reputation for delegation so that they can get on with the high level stuff.

Within a start-up or small business, you do not need delegators. Delegation is a corporate mind-set. You need doers, people who will take responsibility for their own actions, their own development, their own goals, and their own ways of achieving the objectives of the business.

But in hiring this type of person, you once again need to keep in mind the way you work with them. They will not be happy taking orders, or being told 'this is how we do it, final'. They are likely to be almost as creative and enthusiastic as you are, in need of an opportunity to make a difference. Make sure these are the types of people you have in your business, and make sure you understand how best to work with them. This will be covered in more detail in Chapter 14.

Customers and suppliers – their contact is you

When we have worked as senior members of staff in a corporate environment, most of us have been fortunate enough to have a reporting structure in place that allows us to avoid being the key contact person in the business. For example, suppliers will deal with people at a less senior level in the business, and clients can be managed by our direct reports, our own contact limited to what is acceptable.

However people starting their own businesses suddenly become the centre point for all communication. For people with ASD, this can be understandably stressful and difficult to handle. Scott Sheinfeld noted that one of the main differences in the way he needed to work as an entrepreneur as opposed to an executive in the corporate world was 'the constant expectation of people who want to see, talk with or deal with ME directly'. He clarified: 'As an executive, I had watchdogs. It was just understood that vendors and clients and others may not get to speak with me directly. Now my customers expect to get to talk to the owner. I oblige them and am learning to deal with it.'

Some niceties will disappear

Yes, some niceties associated with the corporate world are going to disappear, like formal departments for HR, IT and Marketing. You are unlikely to have specialists working in your business in certain corporate services types of roles, because that is not what your business needs as a start-up or small business. Many of the more essential of these areas can be outsourced (such as payroll, HR and administration), but other areas will require you to just roll up your sleeves and get stuck in. A good example is in the areas of IT. Many small business owners discover they suddenly need to sort out their own IT problems, load their own software, back-up their own machines. Similarly, whereas in the corporate world a manager could leave the HR team to deal with 'problem people', this now becomes something you need to do yourself.

Before you carry on, spend a little time on Toolkit Exercise 3 in Part 5 of the book, thinking about some of the current functions, people and systems you have in the corporate world and considering whether you think these are essentials, nice to haves or luxuries in your own business.

Everyone in the business is 'Marketing'

The one very important change in structure between a corporate and an entrepreneurial business is that there isn't a marketing department, despite this being a critical activity in itself.

When you start up your own business, it is highly likely that you as the business founder are actually going to be the strongest marketing tool for your business. Most of us start our own businesses from the corporate world where we have established reputations and contacts, and so we make use of that to market our ideas.

However, in order for a small business to be successful, it is important that you are not the only person in the business who is focused on marketing the company. Every single employee in a small business or start-up needs to be a formal representative of the business, and have enough knowledge and understanding of what you are doing as an organisation and where you are going to be able to answer questions from potential clients, supplier and financiers. This means that you need to ensure that your goals, activities and plans are transparent for the people in your company, and that they are confident enough to be able to share this should anyone ask them. The best way to do this is to try to build company loyalty – employees who are proud of the company they work with and feel part of the 'family' are the ones who will go out and act as your informal sales reps by talking highly of the company to friends and family.

In the same way that the marketing 'function' will change, so will the way you actually market. As a small business, it is highly unlikely that you will have the budget for formal marketing campaigns, and even if you did, as a small business it is also highly unlikely that these would receive as much interest as a larger company due to the fact that you are smaller and less well known than your competitors. As a result, your efforts need to be far more personal and client specific. For example, don't make the mistake of trying to market by email unless you are emailing a particular customer (or potential customer), and you are offering them something valuable. In general, email marketing is seen as spam, and as such can actually do more harm than good as far as the credibility of your company is concerned.

There are many more areas where there are differences between the corporate world and the entrepreneurial world, but most of these will be covered in the course of the book. What is important for you to keep in mind as someone either thinking about, in the process of or having already made, the move from the corporate world to the entrepreneurial world is that there are differences, and you need to make sure you are open to recognising and acknowledging these in your own business.

PART 3

Practicalities of Starting Up Your Business

Chapter 5

Identifying and Formalising your Business Vision

I've Made the Decision – Now What?

We have already seen that there are many reasons why people make the decision to become an entrepreneur. If you are reading this book, you are probably someone who is still playing with the idea of becoming an entrepreneur: you have made the decision to become an entrepreneur but have not acted on that decision yet, or you are currently an entrepreneur who is seeking some insights. This chapter is largely intended for those people who have made the decision to become an entrepreneur but are not clear on their next steps, or what they need to do in order to have a bit more confidence that they will be able to take on the challenge. However, if you have already started your own business, you will still find this chapter useful.

Identifying your business vision and plan

When you decided to start your own business, you no doubt had an idea of what you would be starting, what the company would do, what it would look like and so forth. The question is whether you have actually put pen to paper in formalising that vision. There are two important considerations in formalising your business vision that are particularly relevant to people on the autism spectrum.

One characteristic of those of us with higher-functioning autism is that we like to get on and do things – if we know what needs to be done, we just want to get on with it. We are passionate about what we see as important, and don't like to waste time on what can be perceived as irrelevant issues. Because of this, we sometimes overlook the critical step of formalising our business vision, and end up down the line with confusion in the organisation about exactly what it is we are trying to achieve.

The second possibility is also related to a strong ASD trait, and that is our focus and attention to detail. If we have decided to draw up a business plan, we sometimes can get into so much detail that we end up creating a 'paper-monster' that never actually comes to life. This scenario is a particularly high risk for those of us leaving the corporate world, since we have been used to developing detailed and extensive business plans as part of that world, yet have had our propensity for great detail bridled by the formal deadlines set by the corporation.

Within an entrepreneurial start-up environment, it is important that the business planning initially involves a Business Vision rather than a detailed Business Plan. OK – so what is the difference between the two?

Business vision versus corporate business plan

When we speak about a business plan, we are describing a formal business document that can be quite detailed. It covers an extensive breakdown of financial plans, research into competitors, opportunities and threats, weaknesses and strengths of the proposed business, and formal marketing, funding and growth strategies. Business plans are intended for corporate level organisations, not for start-ups. As your business grows, you will reach the stage where you will need to develop your own (albeit far less extensive) business plan to use to present to potential funding providers and so forth, and we will speak about this later in the book. However, at this stage in your business set-up, there really is no need for this.

A business vision is usually a one page document which formally states what you see the purpose of your company being, what you intend to offer the market and what your unique selling point or points are. It is your *vision*, and will briefly cover your key goals, how long you expect it to take these to be formally achieved, how many people are going to be involved, and so forth.

While we have said that it is not essential to have a formal business plan at this stage, in starting up something as important as your own business, it is essential that we take the time to do some planning beforehand. Pre-planning is important for any entrepreneur, but I would propose that this is even more important for us. Let me clarify why by referring to some of the work we did in the previous chapter.

When asked to formalise the objectives or goals of their business, most Asperger professionals will confidently advise of a goal that – while seeming daunting to most neurotypicals – is perfectly achievable for us. Examples would include things such as achieving a revenue of one million within the first five years of operation, selling over 5000 units within the first year of trading, or obtaining twelve new clients a month in the first financial year.

All of the above are sound and potentially viable business targets for different types of business operation. However, if we were to share these with people in our new business who were not familiar with our abilities, they would be rather overwhelmed and consider that we were being unrealistic. For this reason, it is important that we bring our planning into a shorter time span, and also turn the focus a little so that there is more of a 'this is how we will do it' feel rather than just seeing the end goal.

This goes back to the challenge of trying to see things through other people's eyes. When we plan and visualise our business goals, we tend to do it for ourselves without taking others into account. As a small business owner it is absolutely essential that we ensure that the vision we have can be shared in a way that neurotypicals can understand, mainly because the majority of people we will deal with are likely to be neurotypical rather than autistic, whether these are employees, clients or potential sources of funding in the future.

What do I need to think about?

Having made the decision that entrepreneurship is for you, there are a number of things that you should do before launching into your business – especially if you are still currently employed and have yet to resign. Most of the more detailed areas that you need to consider and implement are covered later in the book. However, I would like to discuss some specific areas that are important for you to think about ahead of formally starting your business, or drawing up your initial business plans. I am going to introduce a number of templates that you can use as part of your pre-start-up thought processes. Let's start with thinking about what we need to do for ourselves if we are currently still working in the corporate world.

Contracts of employment

If you are currently still working, it is very important that you dig out your original contract of employment and take the time to review it for any potential conflict of interest clauses. Not doing this can result not only in delays in starting your business, but also in potential legal action and significant cost to yourself in terms of both finance and reputation.

Let's have a look at a case study of someone who fell into this trap.

Case study: Jennifer and restraint of trade clause

Jennifer worked as an advisor in the insurance sector, having been employed by a multi-national financial services organisation for over nine years. When Jennifer was passed over for promotion due to a poor performance evaluation in the area of teamwork, she realised that her career aspirations within the large multi-national were unlikely to be met, since her Asperger's meant that teamworking and socialising were not her strongest areas, and yet they were one of main considerations for promotion within her company.

Over the years, Jennifer had started to visualise some ideas for a new service that could be offered to individuals, namely an online pet bereavement counselling service. Although Jennifer struggled to understand and work with people, she had a very strong attachment to animals and knew many people who felt just as strongly about their pets. She had recently lost her favourite cat in a tragic accident, and it had taken her several months to recover from the trauma of the loss of what was literally her best friend. At the time, she had longed to be able to speak with someone who could understand the effects of loss on a person who had such close ties to their pets. However, no such service then existed.

Being a diligent individual, Jennifer did some market research to see how well her idea would go down in the pet-owner community. She contacted a number of veterinary practices to see if they felt there was a need, and also contacted as many pet insurance companies as she could to determine if they offered anything of the sort she was thinking of. Her research told her that this was potentially an excellent business concept, and so she decided to take a leap of faith and resign from her job. Jennifer's manager was not very happy to see her notice being given in, since she was a dedicated and very knowledgeable employee, and to be honest probably did the work of more than one person. He initially tried to convince her to stay by offering her a pay rise but when she said that she was actually leaving to start out in business for herself, he grew angry and insisted on her telling him more details of her ideas. Jennifer was caught unawares, not having expected the negative reaction from her manager, and was quite open about what she intended to do.

Eventually Jennifer came to the end of her notice period, and she made plans to formalise her new business. She registered the business as a private company, and completed all the formalities for revenue and payroll taxes, offices and so forth. She was delighted to find that her idea seemed to be in demand, for with her first quarter of trading, she had more than double the number of clients she had forecast in her initial plans. Then again, she had shared with a number of her clients at her former employer that she was leaving to start her own business, and a number of them had been extremely interested in her service. More than half of her new clients had actually worked with her when she had been employed in the insurance company.

One day, Jennifer received a letter sent to her office by registered mail. She was shocked to discover that her former employer was suing her under a breach of restrictive covenant action from her contract of employment. Jennifer was required to go to court to defend her business and explain her actions.

Looking through her contract of employment with her solicitor ahead of the court hearing, Jennifer was advised that her contract did have a very explicit restraint of trade and non-dealing restrictive covenant clause. According to this, Jennifer could not, for a period of twelve months after leaving the company, either have dealings with any of the clients she had worked with at her previous employment, or undertake any work that could be deemed to be competitive. Jennifer argued that her work was in no way in competition to the standard insurance work being undertaken by her previous employment, but her solicitor did have to agree that the focus of her new business was a form of insurance, as claimed by her previous employer, and that she had explicitly agreed to this clause by signing her contract of employment. In addition, her previous manager had stated that the company had already been discussing starting a pet bereavement service internally by the time Jennifer left, and claimed Jennifer had taken her ideas and contacts directly from these internal discussions.

Jennifer was stressed and shocked. How on earth could her unique and liberating business idea turn into such a nightmare?

The stress that Jennifer experienced had an incredibly negative effect on her ability to continue with her business, even when the courts ruled that her employer was being unreasonable on the 'competition' restrictive covenant, and that the only area that had been breached was the non-dealing covenant.

This situation could have been avoided if Jennifer had done two things – first of all, checked her employment contract for any restrictive covenants that could affect her and taken this into account in her planning, and second, not shared with her manager the full details of her intended business ahead of her leaving the company. The sad reality is that what happened to Jennifer is not such an unusual occurrence, and is an example of another of those concepts we, as people on the spectrum, struggle with – and that is office politics.

Therefore, if you are employed at present and are considering making that exciting move to your own business, make sure you read the small print in your contract of employment. If you are uncertain in any way, check with your legal advisor and just make sure. It is always better to spend a little time and effort ensuring that you are covered before starting your company, rather than finding out after you are trading that there is a problem.

Do I have the resources I need at this time?

When I have prompted people to think about whether or not they have sufficient resources to start their own business, many respond immediately that they have enough money to get their business up and running. However, when I ask the question, 'Do you have the resources you need?' this is intended to cover more than just money.

In starting your own business, there are actually three key resources that it is essential you have sufficient of. The first of these is actually time. Many people make the decision to start their own businesses when they are still working, and often go ahead and start building their business while they are still working their notice. In fact, many people rely on this period of time as an on-going source of income while they do the 'non-revenue generating' activities of starting up their company. However, it does sometimes come as a surprise to them just how much of a time commitment is required for their new business, and frequently they end up making incredible sacrifices to keep their businesses going. This topic will be covered in more detail in Chapter 16.

The second resource is that of money. Yes, we are all aware that we would need funds to start up our business – after all, the business will need things like telephones, email addresses, computers, and so forth. However, there will be regular on-going running costs associated with your business as well as regular personal expenses that you need to ensure you can cover. Remember – you are thinking about the finances needed for your new business *as well as your own personal life and home*. This topic is covered in detail in the following chapter.

The third – and by no means least important – resource is that of knowledge. Intellectual knowledge is indeed a resource, but because it is not something tangible, many people – especially those of us on the autism spectrum – tend to overlook it. Like time, it is not something we can touch or feel, and therefore it can be harder to visualise.

Let's have a look at each of these resources in more detail and think about how best we can ensure that we have the necessary level of resource needed in each to successfully start our business. What follows are some recommendations for when and how to launch your business. It also includes links to some templates in the Toolkit Exercises section of the book, Part 5. In what follows, I have ordered the discussion of the resources linearly, but it is important to recognise that when you sit down and go through the Toolkit Exercises, there will be overlaps between these three resources. For example, you may have to take into account personal time commitments to your family when considering finances, or finances when considering additional knowledge acquisition. However, I have listed them in the order that tends to work optimally. As you work through the templates in Part 5, make sure that you take the time to update those that you completed first with any newly identified issues or insights, as the templates encourage you to do.

Finances

Having sufficient money to start up your business is always going to be an important consideration in deciding when you are ready to start you business, although it has to be said that very often circumstances dictate when we start our businesses rather than pure planning. For example, when I started up one of my more recent businesses, I had been working as a managing director of a company that was moving its headquarters from the UK to the US.

Initially, I had intended to move with the company to the East coast, since I had worked and lived there previously, but events occurring in September 2011 resulted in the company making the strategic decision to move to the West coast instead. This did not suit me, since my daughter was in weekly boarding at the time, being in the middle of her final two years of high school. While it would have been feasible for her to fly over to me on the East coast every other weekend, flying to San Diego just would not have been fair to her.

As a result, I accepted a redundancy package from my employer, and started advising them as an external consultant instead to assist them with the transfer and closure of the UK offices. Word soon got around that I was 'on the market as a consultant' again, and I had companies I had previously worked with contacting me to assist them with change programmes. I made the decision at that time to continue consulting to them through my own business rather than going back into the corporate world straight away, and that is what I did. Stewart, an entrepreneur from the United Kingdom, similarly explains that he was made redundant and hence the decision was ultimately made for him. Aaron, an Australian entrepreneur, found that he was struggling to get a corporate position and – similarly – this as what made the decision for him.

So what are some of the things you will need to consider as far as finances go? I will deal more formally with financial forecasting in the next chapter, but here we are going to take the time to think about your personal finances and what you use. If you have a look at Exercise 4.1 of the Toolkit Exercise 4 in Part 5 of this book, you will find a template for you to review your finances. Can I recommend that you download a copy of this template from www.jkp.com/9781849055093/resources if you are able so that you have a copy of this to hand as I discuss it.

Your first step in completing your template is to think about where you currently are if you are not already operating in your business. You will need to think about such things as what you are getting as a salary after tax, what sort of financial commitments you have personally, and how much you normally spend on those elements that are not regular monthly expenses. As an example, if you have a look at the template in Toolkit Exercise 4, you will see that we have provided a breakdown of some of the most common personal expenses people have. Some of these are once a year costs (such as Christmas or Thanksgiving). In these areas, what you should do is try to realistically work out how much you would normally spend around that time and then divide it by 12. This would give you the average expense allocated equally over the year. Of course, we all know costs don't occur that way. But for the purposes of this exercise, this is fine.

Let me walk through the rest of the template with you. The left hand column contains the descriptions for the fields in the table. We have a section for all of your *personal* income and expenditure, followed by a section for what you have worked out your *company* income and expenditure should be.

Looking at the template, you will see that there are four columns to the right of the description column on the left. These are:

- in your current job
- as a start-up: first thoughts
- as a start-up: thoughts after considering time
- as a start-up: thoughts after considering knowledge

You should start this exercise by completing the *personal* areas under the first column. This column's description is self-explanatory. It is where you should record the income and expenditure you currently experience as an employee, ahead of starting your own business. The section under Business has 'Not Applicable' under the 'In Your Current Job' section, since we are assuming that your business would not have started operating while you are still working full-time. If you are working part-time, however, and your business has already started, I recommend that you start the exercise with the second column, as described below.

The second column is intended to record what you feel your average monthly situation will be like during the first six months of starting your new business. In general, this would mean that you no longer have an income recorded under the *personal* section, but it is recognised that in some cases there may still be some income (for example, if you are working part-time). The second column also allows you to start to consider the company income and expenditure. In this section you need to start thinking about such things as whether or not you need an actual office, or whether you can operate from home. This will make a big difference to your business expenditure, and so I will be discussing it a more a little later.

Now that you have completed the template in Exercise 4.1, it is time to start thinking about some of your other resourcing requirements. For now, do not worry about columns three and four, since they will only be completed later in the toolkit and are explained there.

Time

Time is the second consideration in this exercise. We can have all the money and knowledge in the world, but if we do not have the time to actually start and run a business, we are not going to get anywhere. So let us clarify what we mean when we talk about time, even if this does seem a little obvious.

When we speak about time as a resource, we mean the time that we have available to undertake not only your business related work, but also time required by you as an individual to ensure that you are physically able to continue to run your business. OK – so what do I mean by that? Well, many individuals starting their own companies think about how much time they will need to ensure that the business gets up and running, continues running and has the opportunity to grow. However, they frequently forget that in order for them to be able to operate effectively during this time they need to ensure that their health does not suffer as a result of too many commitments and not enough personal time. Several of the entrepreneurs on the spectrum that I have interviewed have indicated that this was a challenging area for them. Jeremy Samson, Managing Director of Time2Train, says: 'Sometimes it was a challenge just to maintain my health physically, mentally, etc. I sometimes lost track of time and lacked in organising my time appropriately and effectively because I would be having so many creative ideas or stuck on finishing a project that I would lose out on sleep to skipping meals.'

Jeremy's experience is certainly not unique. Asperger traits include our extreme focus and persistence that can be extremely useful in the workplace, but can also create problems for our health. However, in many cases this arises because people just do not realise how much time is required to run their business, or how many other time commitments they already have. Alison Bruning, CEO and Founder of Mountain Springs House, shared her challenges in respect of time commitments:

> The major different [sic] in the way I needed to work as an entrepreneur instead of a worker was the amount of work it would bring. As my business grows so do the demands placed upon me. I have a hard time following my daily routines because of the increased demands place upon me. I never expected that to happen. Sometimes I get overwhelmed by it all. Thankfully, I have my husband. He's been able to take on the finances. That helps a lot.

So in considering launching your own business, it will probably help you to spend a bit of time considering your time commitments at present, and how they could change once you start your own business.

Before you continue reading this chapter, it is essential that you now go to Toolkit Exercise 4 in Part 5 of the book and complete Exercises 4.2 through 4.5 before continuing with this chapter.

Having completed Exercises 4.1 through 4.5, you should now have a better idea of the resources you could potentially have available to you. You will be able to see if there are any areas that could create a challenge for you, such as not having enough time to recharge, and to thereby develop some strategies to deal with this.

Keep in mind that this exercise is not intended to be your final forecast of financial requirements, but is an exercise to give you an initial idea of what resources you will need. The following chapter will help you in doing a more detailed financial forecast once you have actually started your business.

I have done everything mentioned here, but still can't make that first step...

OK, you may argue, I have followed all your advice so far and I am in a good position as far as resources go to start my own business. So why is it that I am struggling to take that first step? There are many reasons why you may be struggling, and it would not be possible for me to advise you on your individual circumstances without knowing the background. However, what I can do is talk about some of the reasons why those of us on the autism spectrum may find it difficult to start our own businesses.

Fear of Change

One of the most obvious reasons why you may be struggling with this decision can be related to a fear of change. Many people on the autism spectrum are very change averse. Routines and consistency are the life-blood of our world, and they are things we will desperately try to conserve in our lives. Taking the decision to leave your corporate job and step out in the entrepreneurial world involves, by definition, a significant amount of change. Surprisingly, it is generally not the fear of entering a risk-taking environment or the way we will have to build a company from scratch that concerns us. It is the fear of change itself that can paralyse us.

There is no simple solution to the challenge of facing the fear of change. I would recommend, however, that you read the final chapter of this book to get some more insights into how to live with change, as well as my other publication *An Asperger Leader's Guide to Living and Leading Change* (Bergemann 2013). I hope these will help you build your confidence in dealing with the insecurities change can cause.

Over-analysing the prospects

Another recognised trait of people on the autism spectrum is that we are very analytical people who go to great depths to get to the bottom of things. This can be a tremendous asset in so many areas. However, it can sometimes act as a hindrance.

When we are enthused about something, we will turn on our almost obsessional focus to delve deeply into that project or situation to find the perfect solution. This can sometimes result in our analysing things to such a detailed extent that we end up putting ourselves off, or find we are never comfortable making a decision. We have over-analysed the situation.

I have explained earlier in this chapter how important it is to make sure that you do not neglect to do some pre-planning and evaluation of your situation before starting your business. At the same time, I now warn you against digging so deep that you are overwhelmed with potential issues or risks that most people would not even have thought about.

If you know yourself to be the type of person who does undertake often overly deep analyses of situations, it may be beneficial for you to set yourself some boundaries. I have found that the best way to do this is write down any concerns you have following your analysis and then allow those concerns to move aside in your mind. If you have recorded them somewhere, they will never be lost, and therefore you can stop focusing on them. Once you have done this, have a look at your vision again and try once more to see if there are any significant challenges. If you continue to come up with arguments against starting your business, or uncertainties about certain elements of it, I can recommend a second course of action. For each of those areas that you have identified as a concern and written down, add three columns next to them, labelled 'High Possibility', 'Reasonable Possibility' and 'Low Possibility'. For each item, then, indicate whether you feel the chance of this issue arising is high, reasonable or low possibility. Having done this, you can immediate put aside anything that you have marked as low possibility. You are not saying that it will never happen, but you are saying that you cannot worry about all possible eventualities, and hence it makes sense to clear from your mind anything that is unlikely to happen.

Next have a look at those areas you marked as having a reasonable possibility of occurring. Consider each one and think about the *effect* of this occurring on you and/or your business. If there is little or no significant effect, add these to the 'put aside' list. If there is a significant or very significant effect, then add these to the 'High Possibility' list. This final high possibility list should now be the only things that you should consider in order to make your decision as to whether to start your own business or not.

Waiting for the manual

Another reason why we sometimes do not take that first step is because we are overly cautious about making our own choices, and are – effectively – looking for the 'how to do it' manual. Much as I would love to say it is, this book is not intended to be your 'how to' manual which covers everything and tells you how and what to do step by step. If you are waiting for the manual to tell you what to do step by step, you aren't really thinking as an entrepreneur.

There is absolutely nothing wrong with looking for some opportunities for personal development through books, coaching and mentorship. However you are ultimately the person who needs to start their business, and every business is different, no matter how alike they appear to be.

Don't wait for a manual that will never appear. Just go out and get started.

Waiting for approval from significant others

The final point I want to mention here relates to a rather sensitive area, but I think it is important to mention it anyway. Some people on the autism spectrum are very dependent on their significant others for approval. Because we struggle to always comprehend the rest of society and the way people think, we rely on these significant others to 'validate' what we are doing so that we do not make a social *faux pas* or create something inappropriate. However, at some point it is important that we step away from our significant others briefly to make the decision about whether or not to start our business by ourselves. Even when the significant other in your life is a partner or spouse, it is really important to make sure that we are the ones making decisions about our lives, rather than those closest to us.

There is nothing wrong with getting feedback and suggestions from those you care about. For us, these are generally the people who understand us the best and can therefore advise us knowing our quirks and challenges. But once you have received that feedback, take it on board along with your own observations and make a decision of your own. Do not sit and wait for approval from anyone. If you do not receive your feedback, go ahead and make a decision by yourself. After all, in running your own business, that will be what you will be expected to do going forward.

Next steps to starting your business

You are now is a better position to consider starting up your business. I will now provide a short check-list of what you should be actively considering as you make the transition. Most of these points are covered later in the book, but some will be specific to your circumstances and your country of residence.

I recommend that you print out a copy of the start-up check-list in Toolkit Exercise 5 in Part 5 (Exercise Table 5.1) and complete it now, and then update it as appropriate as you work through the book.

Chapter 6

Initial Financial Budgeting and Forecasting

Finances for your business

Many corporate executives moving into an entrepreneurial role can be daunted at the prospect of having to draw up their own financial plans or to establish an initial budget for their own company. Many rely on the corporate budgeting skills they learnt as part of their leadership role – reviewing and authorising expenses and costs against detailed and often very complicated financial system cost codes. There are even those who come from a finance background who may find this new level of activity challenging, in that they have never been required to think or operate in a less structured financial environment.

In some respects, coming to grips with the level of financial planning and budgeting required for a start-up small business can actually be easier for an individual who has never done it than for someone who is familiar with it at a corporate level. For those of us who have trained and operated at this level for many years, breaking the habit of formal financial and management accounting for large corporations is easier said than done – even more so for those of us on the autism spectrum.

So in what way is finance and budgeting so different for a small company or start-up?

Financial requirements for small business

I know that many Asperger professionals ask the question 'why should I change my accounting and budgeting practices? Surely if it works for me, and it is a system I know, then that is all that matters?'

The answer to this question is partially that – yes, you need to operate in a way that you are comfortable with. However, by introducing large company thinking, processes and practices into your small company, you will – in all likelihood – change the nature of your role from that of an entrepreneur to an administrator. Let's step back and think about it for a moment. In order to have the elaborate budgeting and cost coding systems that you are used to from within your large company employer, you need a financial system that is larger than you functionally require for a small business. So that is a financial concern. In addition, all of the spreadsheets, reports and data screens you are used to completing and sharing each month actually need to be developed, downloaded or set up. That is a time issue. Above all, you need people to run the reports, upload the data and analyse the reports. That is a resourcing issue. This tells us that having a financial management system that is larger than we actually need to do the job is nothing more than holding onto the practices of the past for no good reason. If you are going to make the move from corporate employment to entrepreneurship, you need to ensure that you embrace entrepreneurial practices, not drag corporate ones with you.

That is not to say, of course, that you can run your business without an adequate financial management system. However, the size and complexity of this will be considerably different. In fact, depending on the size and nature of your business, you may actually completely outsource your financial management to your accountancy provider, operating any internal information on Excel sheets provided to and from your outsourcing company.

There are many very useful books on budgeting and financial planning for small businesses out there, so I do not intend to focus too extensively on the nuts and bolts of this topic. However, it is important for you to be aware of some of the minimum requirements in the area of finance for you as an entrepreneur opening your business – especially for those people who have no experience in this field at all. For this reason, the following section gives a very brief outline of what you need to ensure you understand and can work with on the budgeting and finance side. This is intended for those people who are not really familiar with finance and budgeting. If you are fairly familiar with the concepts here, please feel free to skip this section.

Terminology you need to understand

As part of Chapter 5 you undertook an exercise to get an idea of the financial requirements of starting up your business. This is useful for determining if it is the right time for you to launch your business, but is not sufficient for you to prepare your business plan formally. If you are going to do such things as opening bank accounts and obtaining credit, you will need to have a little more of a financial statement that you can share with your potential credit providers.

Let's start by having a look at some of the terminology and concepts in finance and accounts that it is absolutely essential you understand as a business owner. Keep in mind that the terms I am using are general accounting terms, but in some countries the name may change slightly (for example, Cost of Sales can be called Cost of Goods Sold, and so forth). However, you should be able to recognise the terms from the description I have given. The most important thing is that you understand what they mean. It is important to keep in mind as well that these descriptions refer to the meanings as they apply to a business, not an individual.

Assets

These are the things that your company owns that have value and are used in the course of your business, generally as part of generating income. Examples would include things like machinery, office equipment, vehicles, and so forth.

Liabilities

This is what your company owes to others (known as the company's creditors). This includes things such as loans, overdrafts and credit accounts.

Income

This is the total amount of money that the business earns during a defined period of time, generally the financial year of the company.

Cost of sales

These are all the costs that are as a direct result of providing your service or making your product. If you are a service company, this will include things like the cost of consultant salaries, costs of presentation material, travel to clients, and so on. If you have a product, this is likely to include the cost of raw materials, salaries of manufacturing staff, and so forth. Indirect costs such as operations, marketing and distribution are not included in this.

Expenses

These are the payments that the company makes in the course of a financial period. This includes things such as office rental, stationery, distribution costs and general salaries.

Profit

The profit of a business is the amount of money the company has left over when all expenses, cost of sales and taxes have been deducted. It is effectively the amount of money that the company 'takes home'.

There are also four important types of report or analysis that you need to be aware of, since these are frequently what your creditors would ask you for if you are applying for credit.

Balance sheet

People considering extending credit to you business will want to understand what you owe and what you own that can be sold to cover that liability should the need arise. This is reflected by what is known as a balance sheet. It is a summary of your company's assets, liabilities and equity. Equity is the amount that you have when you deduct total liabilities from total assets. It represents the overall value of the company should it be closed at any point in time.

Profit and loss statement

While the balance sheet is useful in understanding the overall value of the business, the profit and loss statement breaks down the information into much more detailed areas. It is basically a summary of the income and expenses of the business over a period of time, broken down into the main areas of spending. So, for example, the profit and loss statement shows exactly how much was spent on salaries, business entertaining, telephones, stationery, and so on. It is very useful if a potential creditor wants to have a better understanding of how your income is being spent, and whether it is being properly managed.

Breakeven analysis

A breakeven analysis literally shows the cut-off point between making a profit and making a loss. We say that a business breaks even if the amount of money it earns in sales is enough to cover its expenses.

Cash flow forecast

A cash flow forecast predicts how money will come into the business and how it will go out over a period of time. Cash flows are generally split up into operational cash flow (money from sales and operating expenses), investment income and expenditure and financing income and spending (relating to financing from banks, owners, etc.).

The good news for you if you are not a particularly financially minded person is that it is not necessary for you to be the person who draws these financial statements up once your business is up and running. Your accountant generally does this for you. However, it is extremely important for you to understand what these financial statements mean so that if you are spoken to about them, you can give an educated answer. On the other hand, you may need to draw up elementary versions of these as part of your business plan when applying for credit. I will cover this scenario in more detail for you in Chapter 8. However, for now I want to focus the rest of the chapter on what you need to ensure you have considered up front as far as your finances are concerned.

Developing your first budget

Now that you have decided to start your business, you will need to think about drawing up your first budget to ensure that you have the money available to see you through. Many people underestimate the importance of establishing a budget, generally because they feel that they have a good idea of the money they have and what expenses they are likely to incur ahead of earning any income, and therefore they can manage. However, in reality it is far better to spend a little time actually drawing up a budget so that you have a better idea of how your money is going to be spent exactly over the months to come, as well as to draw up a contingency plan for if income is not received when it is expected.

Budgets are extremely useful tools for ensuring control of the money moving through your business, as well as for giving you better insights into just how many commitments you have to which income needs to be allocated.

In Toolkit Exercise 6 in Part 5 of the book, you will find a template for an elementary budget that can be used by you to try to work out how you are going to spend your money invested in the business over the coming year. It is important that you do make provision for unexpected expenses in the first month, and carry forward any unspent monies into the following month, together with any debts you have that you have yet to pay.

If you have a look at this template, you will see that it is broken down into four periods. Generally, this is because in accounting we tend to report financial information on a quarterly basis, so every three months in the year. However, you may well want to develop your budget on a monthly basis, in which case the four periods would represent four consecutive months. The budget form, therefore, can be adapted to suit your needs.

You will also see that I have included several expense areas on the sheet. If some of these are not relevant to you, you can leave them blank. On the other hand, if there are some areas that you feel are additional expenses (or income) that you should record, there is space to add these in.

I suggest you end this chapter by having an initial look at the budgeting spreadsheet in Toolkit Exercise 6 and seeing how much you are able to complete.

Chapter 7

Developing a Competitive Advantage

So we have an idea, we have decided to start our own business and we are ready to go. What are some of the important things we need to keep in mind as we begin our journey into the land of the entrepreneur? There are some important considerations when it comes to entering the marketplace with a new company offering a product or service, and the nature of these considerations is dependent on whether what you are offering is a new concept in the marketplace, or whether you are offering a variation on an already existing theme.

Ways to enter the market as a new business

When you enter the market, there are a couple of ways you can do this. You could be starting your business because you have come up with a completely new product or service for the marketplace, such as a type of technology that does not currently exist or a service that has never been offered. Examples of this are the development of the cellular phone, which was a completely new product at the time, or the introduction of the first virtual accountancy system.

The second way you can enter the market is as someone offering a variation on a current product or service already available. Examples would be the introduction of the Dyson vacuum cleaner. The vacuum cleaner had been around as a product for many years, but James Dyson created a variation on that standard product that was unique and therefore highly valuable. An example of a variation on a service theme can be found when we consider some of the services offered by banks. In order to deal with the banks, we used to have to go into the branches and do everything face-to-face. Then the concept of online banking was introduced, and this produced a whole new service based on an existing service we were already familiar with, but which offered so much more.

In thinking about your business concept, it is very important for you to consider whether what you are starting is a new concept or variation on a theme, and you will understand why this is so important as you continue with this chapter. If you believe that what you are offering is new, do take the time to undertake some formal market research to ensure that your perceptions are correct.

Let's look now at some important considerations in bringing a completely new product into the market.

Introducing a new concept to the market

Contrary to popular belief, bringing a completely new concept to the market is not always the easiest option for new businesses. You would think that if you have a great idea and no other competition in the marketplace, this would mean that introducing the business product or service would be far easier. In reality, in the majority of cases it can be far harder. There are a number of reasons for this:

- Despite our being well aware of the value of what we are introducing to the market, new concepts are frequently treated with suspicion by consumers, who tend to want to see how it works for 'others' before investing themselves.

- When we introduce a new concept to the market, competition is likely to develop very soon thereafter, as competitors seek to offer alternative products or services with more unique qualities.

- By being the pioneer in the marketplace for a new concept, we need to ensure we are constantly developing the product to ensure it always continues to lead the market as the market begins to have more competition.

That said, we also need to recognise the advantages of being a company that brings something new to the market:

- Provided the product or service is introduced to the marketplace in an appropriate manner, there is the potential for your business to obtain a lot of free publicity and 'air-time'.

- You are the ones who set the pricing strategies in the beginning, meaning that – even if down the line you may need to review your costing structure – initially this will be set at optimal levels.

- As the first and only provider of the commodity in the marketplace, you have the potential to obtain a very valuable market share in the beginning ahead of other competitors joining the market.

- There is the potential to make your business name synonymous with the particular market itself.

- You can also potentially have an advantage when it comes to the recruitment of the best people working in the area concerned (if there is related technology or intellectual knowledge).

- Your company can retain their leadership or market presence by applying for patents on key ideas and concepts.

I think you can see from the above there are certainly a number of good reasons to introduce a new commodity to the market, provided that this is done in an appropriate manner, with awareness of some of the things to avoid. So just what are some of the considerations you should take into account if you are starting your own business based on a new commodity?

Research consumer needs

One of the most important considerations for us as people on the spectrum is that while we are often incredibly insightful when it comes to the potential of a new concept or idea, we are not always so insightful when it comes to linking that to the receptiveness of the public, largely due to the fact that we struggle with seeing things from the perspective of others.

Ensure optimal timing

We also tend to want to get things going as soon as we can, wanting to share our excitement and enthusiasm with everyone. However, it frequently happens that there are very important timing considerations in launching a new product that may necessitate our waiting for a more optimal time to actually go live. Launching something as soon as possible just to get a product out there is not always the best solution. Make certain that you take the time to do some research together with being aware of current events that could influence your product or service launch.

Sometimes being the best is more important than being the first

It isn't always the best strategy to focus all your attention on being the first to market with a product or service. There are many entrepreneurs who have rushed to launch a new business based on a new product or service in order to be the first to market, only to lose share very quickly to other companies that introduce a more superior product, purely because they took the time to do some customer research and product development.

As mentioned earlier, it is true that being the first to market with a unique commodity can be beneficial, but this is only the case if you are also able to offer the customer something of value. Remember that the moment you bring your product to the market, others will be trying to produce something better as competitors to you. Being first to market is synonymous with continuously working to maintain your competitive edge.

Offering a variation on a theme

The second way to enter the market is to introduce a variation on a currently existing product or service. This variation may be in the form of some new element of an existing commodity, or it could be a variation in the form of a significant increase in value or quality for the customer.

The important thing to keep in mind for the entrepreneur trying to obtain a competitive advantage this way is that you also ensure that the value you introduce into the marketplace through your new product or service is on-going and consistent. This means that you need to ensure that the value of your product to the client is regularly assessed.

These are the sorts of things that you should keep in mind as you start reading Chapter 8, which will guide you in developing a formal business model and plan for your business.

Chapter 8

Developing a More Formal Business Model and Plan

By now you will probably have a clearer picture of the optimal form of your proposed business and have also started to take your first steps towards actually starting it up. One characteristic of those of us with an autism spectrum disorder is that we like to get on and do things – if we know what needs to be done, we just want to get on with it.

As detailed in Chapter 5, when asked to formalise the objectives or goals of their business, most people on the autism spectrum will confidently advise of a goal that – while seeming daunting to most neurotypicals – is perfectly achievable for us. Additional examples would be stating you would achieve 200 per cent of forecast income for the year, or delivering all projects ahead of schedule.

All of the above are sound and potentially viable business targets for different types of business operation, and as people on the spectrum, there is a high possibility that we would be able to achieve these targets if we set our minds to it. These are valuable vision statements for us to use as part of our initial development of our visions statement, as described in Chapters 5 and 6. However, as our business grows and becomes more established, there are a couple of things we need to consider in continuing to use these sorts of targets.

The first consideration is that we are setting objectives which will ultimately have an effect on other employees in our business. While these sorts of targets may seem perfectly achievable to us, to our employees they may be overwhelming.

The second consideration is that the targets we set will be observed by those organisations we may approach for funding. If they cannot see how we have come to set such high objectives, it is unlikely that they would be willing to invest in our company.

A final consideration is that we may very well be setting targets for our small business based on some of our corporate thinking. By this, I mean that we may not take into account that we do not have the corporate resources behind us that we would require to achieve these targets.

The best way to ensure we cover all these things is to pull together a business plan that covers some of your thinking about how you can achieve your targets. As I have said previously, my focus is not the technical side of pulling together a business plan or financial statement. Rather, it is on those areas which may well be challenging for those of us on the spectrum. Hence, I am not going to go into a lot of detail on the financial side, but will talk you through an elementary business plan and how to ensure you cover areas that may not naturally be part of your thinking. In addition, I want to make sure that you do not end up trying to re-create a corporate business plan but develop one which is appropriate for a small business.

Components of an entrepreneurial business plan

There are seven sections of a business plan that are essential for a small or start-up business. These are:

- business profile
- market analysis
- description of your product or service
- sales and marketing plans and targets
- operating plan
- financial plan
- action plan.

Business profile

Your business plan needs to open by describing your business and who you are. Describe details of when you started, who the leadership team is, the size of the company and why you decided to enter the market. Mention the format of the business: for example, is it a partnership, a limited company, a charity? It is important to include relevant information about the people starting up the company (namely yourself and other partners), but not information that is 'nice to have'. So having a business degree and 15 years' experience is important to include, but information such as your education in a completely different field is not so relevant. Always consider the reader as if he was you: what would I want to know about someone coming to join my business?

Market analysis

Your business plan needs to contain a section describing the market that you are intending to – or have already – entered. What is the situation in that market at present? Why have you decided to enter it? Are there gaps in the market you are intending to fill? Who are your main competitors and how does your product/service add value over their offering?

This serves two purposes. First, it shows any potential investor that you have researched and understand your market. Second, it helps you to keep in mind your competitors and what you need to focus on in order to ensure you have a competitive advantage.

Depending on your business, the market background may be a particularly long section of your document. However, do keep in mind that you are now doing a piece of work at the level of a small business. Do not try to enter everything to the extensive level of a corporate business plan. You need to research to the level you would be operating, not them.

Description of your product or service

Your plan must formally explain what your product/service is and what differentiates it from what is already out there in the marketplace. What are the key selling points? Once again, do not create a ten-page section that goes into technical detail of a product. Remember that your readers are unlikely to be technical people and do not want to see that level of information. This is more of a detailed summary. Just ensure that you include essential information as outlined above.

Sales and marketing plans and targets

There are two aspects to sales and marketing here, and I will deal with them separately.

MARKETING STRATEGY

Under this heading outline how you intend to market your product or services. I speak about this in Chapter 11, so you may find it helpful to complete this only once you have read through that part of the book. Marketing as a small business is very different to marketing as a corporate, and is far more focused on you. Therefore, the marketing strategy section is going to be far more succinct than you would expect it to be in a corporate business plan. Most of the time you will include details of where you intend to market your services, when and using what resources.

SALES PLANS AND TARGETS

This is a far more relevant and important section for you. In this part of your document, detail what you are expecting in respect of sales of your product. A corporate business plan, as those of you from a corporate background know, generally includes short-term (6 months–1 year), medium-term (2–3 years) and long-term plans (3–5 years). In an entrepreneurial business you should not be planning this far ahead. As I have mentioned before, your planning needs to be far more adaptive than this, because you will be making decisions on a far more regular basis in respect of your business. Therefore, your plan should really be focused on the 6-month period, with 12–18 months being considered your long-term strategy. The same applies to your sales plans. You need to elucidate on how you see sales being achieved within those periods, and then support this by the detailed breakdown of your targets.

Operating plan

This part of the plan tells the reader how you intend to operate your business. It will cover such things as whether you have a physical office, a virtual office or a factory. It will talk about resources you intend to use, namely your staff, your equipment and your facilities. You should also briefly talk about how you intend to manage any risks that you may have identified in setting up your business: for example, how are you planning to handle services to clients if you are taken ill? This is usually done by a brief SWOT analysis. SWOT is an abbreviation of Strengths, Weakness, Opportunities and Threats. Provide short (but honest) details of your business's strengths, its weaknesses, what opportunities there are for your business in particular and what threats there are.

Once again, I emphasise that this is not intended to be a detailed breakdown of all your systems, process and structures. It is a detailed summary, with perhaps more detail in areas that are particularly important, such as handling risks.

Financial plan

As I said earlier on, it isn't my intention in this book to go into a lot of detail about financial analysis. That said, this section of your plan should contain information for the current statement of your business that you may well have been able to establish from the exercises you did in Chapters 5 and 6. If you go online, you will be able to see a number of very useful templates for small business financial planning sheets that are appropriate for business plans. Make sure that you do search for something for small businesses, though, or you will end up finding templates that ask for far too much information.

The second part of this is to provide a forecast of how you see your finances over the coming period (using 12–18 months as your long-term plan). It is also important to explain any areas in the forecast which may cause concern, such as periods where sales are lower, or expenses higher, as well as ensuring that your projections are realistic. It is always good for you as an individual to be optimistic and set yourself challenging targets. However, what you put in your business plan needs to be seen as realistic and achievable. Keep in mind that your plan will be read by neurotypical people who do not necessarily understand our ability to go into 'super-achievement' mode!

Action plan

As the final section of your plan, your action plan summarises how you intend to use all your detailed strategies in your day-to-day business. It provides a bit more granularity around how you intend to achieve what you have set out above. It would link targets to specific people and timeframes, and it would clarify what the objectives are for some defined periods of time. I find this particularly useful for sharing with my teams in the business, and agreeing this with them, since it can be the basis against which you determine whether you and your team have achieved their objectives for the month or quarter.

It can be seen from the above action plan that some parts of your business plan are not static. Your plan should be considered a dynamic document, far more so than for a corporate, meaning that you update and review this on a regular basis. As your business grows and learns, so your plan will change at the same time: targets could change, marketing strategies could change, and so forth. Without a doubt your action plan will change, but make sure this is not the only area of the plan that gets reviewed on a regular basis.

Additional considerations for those on the spectrum

There are a couple of points I would like to add that are specific to those of us on the spectrum.

Make it realistic for a neurotypical reader

As I have already mentioned, it is important to ensure that you develop the document with strategies and targets that do not make the reader think that you are being unrealistic. We all know that the often challenging targets (in neurotypical terms) that we set are related to our ability to operate in a different way to neurotypicals. However, most people reading your document just will not understand that.

For example, I am one of those people on the spectrum who actually requires very little sleep, hence I tend to sleep for four hours a night or less. As a result I have a lot more time available to me than most neurotypicals who on average need seven hours sleep a night. When people see the number of things I have committed to during the day, they often come back to me with the retort that it is 'physically impossible' to do that amount of work. My immediate response would of course be that it may be for them, but it certainly isn't for me. However, I do tend to keep that sort of reply to myself.

Instead, I tend not to share the details of everything I need to do or want to do. In drawing up your plans, consider a friend or family member who is neurotypical. Ask yourself the question, 'If they had the same amount of knowledge as me, do I think they would be able to do what I am putting in this plan without difficulty?' If your answer is, 'No – they would run out of time,' or something similar, you need to consider revising your plan.

You can do this in two ways. Lower your targets to a neurotypical level (resulting in you being able to over-achieve against your targets), or add in an additional resource. This could be someone already in your resource plan that you just 'increase accountability' for. In reality, you would probably still be doing the work. My preference is for the first option, since it allows you to reflect that you are meeting and exceeding the identified targets and objectives of the business.

Don't try to be corporate in your writing

Particularly for those of you coming from a corporate background, make sure that you do not make the mistake of trying to write a business plan in 'corporate speak'. As members of the corporate world, we all learn the appropriate terminology and nomenclature for our organisation. However, this is frequently totally inappropriate for a small business. In a small business, your plan needs to be in a far more informal format. I am not saying that it needs to be completely informal, but it often reads better if it becomes a first-person document. So as an example, instead of writing 'The business leadership will determine the operating model to be used in the human resources department is that of the Ulrich model' you would write 'We feel that the best model for our human resources team is the Ulrich approach'. Can you see the subtle difference?

This can be a team effort

Another big difference that you may struggle to adapt to is that when drawing up a business plan for a small business with only a few key employees, it is acceptable to draw this up as a team. Within the corporate world this is territory of the leadership team alone, and people within the business as a whole just would not get to be involved. In your small business, the best way to get people committed to the business is to involve them in drawing up the plan. Your people will then feel far more a part of your vision, and will end up being far more motivated. In fact, if you draw it up alone, you are far more likely to create negative feelings, since people would potentially perceive you as trying to distance yourself from your team.

Above all else, this is an excellent opportunity for you to start building some relationships with your team, something covered in more detail later in the book. It gives your staff an opportunity to share their ideas with you, and for you to let them see that you take their ideas into consideration. This is a key component of building the respect of your team.

A final point on this would be that you must always remember that, while you are building the plan as a team, you are the final decision maker in respect of the final version. You need to make it clear from the start that you want to develop this plan together since you value the insights of your team, and once all input has been shared, you will sign it off. It is still important for people to feel you are in charge and in control, not that you are asking for their assistance because you don't know what to put in the plan.

Chapter 9

The Entrepreneur as a Leader

When one thinks about becoming an entrepreneur, most people have a vision of an independent, confident individual who goes out there and makes things happen. To some extent that is perfectly correct: a successful entrepreneur is someone who is willing to take those bold steps into the unknown and create a new business out of nothing. However, there is one part of that vision that actually tends to be slightly different in reality. For most entrepreneurs, they really are not acting independently; they are becoming leaders of a small company. This is an important consideration for those of us on the autism spectrum intending to become an entrepreneur – becoming an entrepreneur means becoming a leader.

When I talk about being a leader as an entrepreneur, I am not only speaking about being a leader of people. Now that may sound confusing, but as you read further, this will become clear. So in what ways is an entrepreneur a leader?

1. *Entrepreneur as leader of ideas* – An entrepreneur needs to be someone who is a leader in ideas. By this, I mean that the entrepreneur needs to be someone who uses his or her intuition and creativity to visualise unique solutions, opportunities and products. They cannot be the sort of personality who relies purely on facts and the analytical application of knowledge. While this may be useful when their creative ideas are implemented, it does not help to create the ideas in the first place.

2. *Entrepreneur as leader of decisions* – This may sound like an unusual thing to say, but it is an important consideration as far as entrepreneurship is concerned. As an entrepreneur you will be the key decision maker in your business, and therefore you need to have the ability to be bold enough to take decisions, even if they are not popular ones. A successful entrepreneur is someone who is confident enough to take control of situations and sort them out by taking key decisions.

3. *Entrepreneur as leader of people* – This tends to be the definition of leadership that we are most familiar with. An entrepreneur is someone who leads the people in his or her company, and provides visible direction to them. The most successful entrepreneurs tend to be those who are enthusiastic in front of their staff despite the circumstances, since people working around them tend to follow their lead and get caught up in that enthusiasm.

4. *Entrepreneur as leader of themselves* – So what do I mean by this? Entrepreneurs are people who can motivate themselves, and who are not reliant on the encouragement of other people to deliver results. By definition, entrepreneurs tend to be relatively independent, and as such they do not have the resources to support and encourage them that someone working in a corporate environment, or even studying, would have. Entrepreneurs need to believe in themselves and know how to encourage themselves when the going gets tough.

Now that we have outlined the areas of leadership, let's think about how this can be of particular importance for people with an autism spectrum disorder. Let's start with the definition of an entrepreneur being a leader of ideas.

Asperger leaders as leaders of ideas

There is no doubt that people on the autism spectrum can be considered very creative people by neurotypical standards. We tend to see things differently, and this unique view of the world can provide us with the capacity to create some very unique things. At the same time, however, we can also be very strongly attached to analysing data and going with the facts. From a neurotypical perspective this can be seen as a contradiction; for us it is just how our minds work.

In order for us to be successful in this element of entrepreneurial leadership, it is essential that we do not allow ourselves to get tied into the detailed analytical mode of thinking. We need to ensure that we regularly check what we are doing to see if there has started to be an emphasis on that side of things to the detriment of the creative, or that our creative ideas are not being stifled because we are trying to make them fit into a pre-existing pattern.

The most successful ASD entrepreneurs are those who have been able to utilise these two different skills in tandem, an example of which can be seen in the comment from Steward Rapley, a British entrepreneur. 'I can develop my own vision,' he says, 'My intense focus on spotting "inconsistencies" and "misalignments" means that I am a good problem-solver. I tend to get in and sort things out in quite a radical, effective way – and spot what is going on quite quickly.'

On the other hand, when these do not work well together, this can create problems for us, as indicated by Alex, an entrepreneur from the US. He says: 'Some challenges are 1) focusing too hard on one task, or worse, a particular worry of a personal nature which distracts me; 2) thinking too far ahead in the future obstructs my energy from concentrating on the present and making the most of it; 3) everything needing to be perfect and when it isn't, self-criticism or walking away.'

An example of where this hasn't worked relates to a lady by the name of Cassie.

Case study: Cassie's cellular travel guide

Cassie was a young woman who had always wanted to start her own business. She had always struggled to fit into the workplace due to her Asperger's and she felt that, despite having a lot to offer an employer, she was being restricted in her career development.

One day, she discussed with her brother an idea she had been contemplating relating to the development of a live travel guide that could be downloaded as an application on people's cellular phones, and which could provide 'live' information relative to where they were, based on the GPS signal on their phone. The idea was a new one, and her brother agreed that this was something that could 'take the market by storm'. Not being a technical person, he agreed to join her in her business in return for some financial investment.

Cassie started development of the product immediately. She was excited by the prospect of introducing the product to the market and potentially developing her new company within a short period of time. However, after an initial period of intense development, Cassie started to spend more and more time testing her product and undertaking market research to determine exactly what it was that customers would value. Cassie's brother warned her that she needed to concentrate on getting the product out into the marketplace, since he had already been speaking as part of his networking sessions, and people were taking note of the idea. However, Cassie was more interested in making sure that the cellular screenshots were as perfect as they could be, and that the scripts on the screens read as simply as possible.

Despite her brother's concerned nagging, Cassie continued to focus on the front-end of the product – the bigger picture of being the first product of this type in the marketplace disappearing into the background.

One day Cassie's brother came storming into her office. 'Look at this!' he snapped, throwing a newspaper onto her desk. Cassie picked it up and read the advertisement on the page in horror. One of the cellular phone network providers had just launched a new product – a cellular phone based travel guide that provided live information using the phone's GPS tracker… Her brother was furious.

'I told you this would happen,' he growled. 'It's always the same. You come up with a great idea, then you get your head stuck into the details and the vision flies out the window!'

Cassie's focus on the detailed analysis of her product meant that she totally lost sight of the bigger picture – that creative vision she had initially had. Cassie was also more fortunate than a lot of people in that she had her brother there to warn her about what she was starting to do. What would have made the difference in this case would have been Cassie taking note of her brother's warning and making a conscious effort to step back from the detail.

In order to ensure that you do not fall into the same trap as Cassie, it is always advisable – if possible – to have someone working with you who can alert you to the fact that you are becoming analytical instead of visionary. Of course, not everyone can have this. In this case, what I recommend is that you start each day by reading through your vision statement for your business, then determining what you need to achieve in the day relative to that vision. At the end of the day, take some time to review what you have spent your time doing, and whether or not this has been 'visionary' or 'analytical'. If you find that you have started to spend more time doing analytical work, it may be worthwhile getting some input from your team. Ask them what the vision of the business is and what you are aiming to achieve strategically. Hear from them what they understand your vision to be. I find this to be remarkably re-orientating.

Asperger leaders as leaders of decisions

For some people on the spectrum, the realisation that owning your own business makes you the central decision maker can be difficult. Jeremy Samson, Managing Director of Time2Train highlights this concern as he shared the following about the differences he found in working as an entrepreneur versus a corporate employee: 'Learning to accept and understand followed by coping with the reality that every responsibility is solely mine. This sometimes became a little overwhelming especially without any support.'

Jeremy's comments echo a lot of ASD people's concerns about being the sole decision maker. Especially for people who have lived in an environment at home where many decisions have previously been made for them, this can be particularly challenging.

At the other end of the scale, there are many people on the spectrum who become entrepreneurs and happily start making decisions about the business. However, these people can sometimes do so to the detriment of the rest of the organisation, turning the business into a 'one-man band' rather than a proper business. A leader who never lets his team have any input into decisions being made is ignoring the next key element of entrepreneurial leadership, and that is leading people. People in a small business need to feel that they are part of the company, that they have an input and are valued. If you end up making decisions without involving anyone, you will find resentment developing among your team and that your best people ultimately leave.

'Wait,' you may ask, 'so this means I have to be the sole decision maker and yet not make all the decisions?' No, not really. What I am saying is that as an entrepreneurial leader, the ultimate decision on anything sits with you. That does not mean that you go and make decisions without consulting with anyone else. Quite the opposite. It means that – after a subject has been discussed and various options proposed by members of your team – you are the one who gets make the final decision.

Part of this also involved being able to stand by your decisions, and make a stand when you have made your choice.

Asperger leaders as leaders of themselves

This element of entrepreneurial leadership is often seen as a particular area of strength for people on the spectrum, but it does have the potential to create a challenge for some people as well. It is well known that the majority of people with autism spectrum disorder prefer to work alone, are highly focused in what they are doing and know how to motivate themselves. However, what is also recognised is that we also tend to be very hard on ourselves, frequently 'beating ourselves up' when things do not go perfectly. I think anyone on the spectrum will agree with me when I say we really aren't the type of people who cheer ourselves on mentally with cries of 'Go, boy, go – you can do it!' However, we have a deeply ingrained need to be and do the best that we can, and this translates into a form of motivation for us.

As mentioned above, one area that we do need to be aware of is the tendency for some of us to be very hard on ourselves and as a result suffer from depression quite easily. Tony Attwood (2007) says 'People with Asperger's syndrome appear vulnerable to feeling depressed, with one in three having a clinical depression… People with Asperger's syndrome are often perfectionists, tend to be exceptionally good at noticing mistakes, and have a conspicuous fear of failure' (pp.140–141). As an entrepreneurial leader, it is essential that we do not make the mistake of being overly critical of ourselves, and thereby running the risk of falling into a negative mindset.

Important implications of being an entrepreneurial leader

The first point that I would like to make is that there is a distinct difference between leadership within a corporate environment and that within a small business. Leadership in a corporate is all about power, authority and distance from the front-line. A leader in this environment is generally set apart to a certain extent from the day-to-day operations of the business and the people doing this work. A corporate leader makes decisions and communicates these to the business through a series of managers – frequently several organisational layers of them. They have a significant amount of support and resources, including things such as personal assistants and administration teams.

When you become an entrepreneurial leader, the vast majority of the above falls away. No longer do you have the resources and support you previously had, and no longer do you communicate through your managers. You are no longer set apart from the business and its operations, but are far more hands-on and involved with the day-to-day activities. While you most certainly still have the same level of authority – if not more – there are subtle differences in the concept of control. Now you need to work far closer with your teams in order to keep them motivated through inclusion, and it is no longer sufficient to just make corporate level decisions without consulting your teams. There is no such thing as an 'executive committee' as such – you are the executive and your small business team is the rest of your committee!

If you have come from a corporate background, you are going to have to make the change in mindset from corporate to entrepreneurial in as far as leading your people is concerned. You will be required to be a lot closer to the business and to get involved in the day-to-day activities, communication and more social elements of your business. From the perspective of someone on the spectrum, what this means is that you need to invest some time in your people skills, something I have covered under Chapters 14 and 15 on building relationships in the workplace and networking.

Another difference, as pointed out earlier, is that you will be more hands on in respect of your decision making, and therefore will need to make those decisions at a much 'lower level' than you may perhaps have been used to. Sometimes this can initially cause frustration as individuals question why they have to start deciding what they consider to be 'basic' things that they are used to a report dealing with in their prior corporate career. As I say, entrepreneurship is hands-on, not elite. In most cases, however, this tends not to be such an issue for people on the spectrum in the long term, since we tend to take ownership of any new challenge. What may actually become a challenge, though, is that we may end up taking too much ownership. What do I mean by this?

As indicated above, when we first start our own businesses, we discover that we have to take decisions at a very detailed level. Once we have started to do this, we can run the risk that once we start to grow our new business, we fail to then allow the decision making to filter back down to other employees, effectively causing bottlenecks due to insisting that everything goes through us. In other words, we fail to delegate once we have the staff. Think about it this way. We have made the change in mind-set from corporate leader to entrepreneur and as a result have changed our level of decision making. This was challenge number one. Once we got used to working that way, our business then started to grow and we brought people on board. But to change our way of making decisions again so soon is a further challenge and sometimes one we resist even more than the first change – not only because it is the second change, but because we have now taken ownership of this as our new focus and it is very hard to let go again. Do remember the well-known phrase 'Don't do – delegate' at this stage. While it may have been reversed when you initially started up (to 'don't delegate – do'!) once your business is growing you need to let go.

Asperger leaders as leaders of people

This is perhaps the most challenging element of entrepreneurial leadership for us. Many people on the spectrum are challenged by having to deal with people and the associated communication with them. I am not going to cover this element further here, since it is the focus of Chapter 14.

In working with individuals in an entrepreneurial environment your contacts will not only be restricted to those within your organisation. As an entrepreneur, you will need to ensure that you develop optimal working relationships with your business suppliers – and if you have come from a business leadership background, the nature of this relationship is not going to be the same as the one you are used to. Let us go into this in some more detail in Chapter 10.

Chapter 10

Dealing with Suppliers

Dealing with suppliers can still present us with some challenges as people on the autism spectrum.

I am speaking here about suppliers that offer us credit accounts. I am not really concerned with those suppliers you work with on a cash basis. But when you need to establish credit accounts, there are things you need to take into account. If you have come from a corporate background, you will no doubt already be experienced in dealing with vendors or suppliers. However, you will find that in dealing with the same community as a small business owner rather than a corporate executive, the way you communicate with them will subtly change. Therefore, I would say that the contents of this chapter are as relevant for you as they are for someone undertaking this activity for the first time.

Initial contact – setting up business supplier accounts

As a small business owner, one of the things that you will need to do quite early on in the life of your business is to set up some supplier accounts. If you have come from a corporate background, you will probably consider this to be rather a straightforward activity. This is understandable, since as a corporate executive you generally have several suppliers actively pursuing you in trying to win your business. Corporates are juicy meals for suppliers, and they will go out of their way to try to offer you all they can, and appear as congenial as possible in order to win your business. This makes things so much easier for us – we have our choice of who we want to work with and under what conditions. Sometimes, in fact, this is all done for us by our procurement teams, and the only contact we have with our suppliers is at our own discretion. For most of us on the spectrum, that is a significant bonus, since we do not really enjoy the people side of supplier relationships.

However, when you are setting up supplier accounts as a start-up, things are very different. First of all, we do not have a procurement team to negotiate and set up contracts for us. Second, suppliers are unlikely to come to us: we need to approach them. Unlike in the corporate world where we are doing them a favour by using them, in a start-up situation this scenario is totally reversed – the suppliers are doing us a favour in allowing us to set up an account with them. So whereas in a corporate world we would be expecting the suppliers to pull out all the stops and practically woo us into working with them, in our start-up world, we would be proving to them that we are worthy of their credit. It is a very different way of communicating.

So what are some of things we need to keep in mind when setting up supplier contracts as a start-up business? Well, if you are coming from a corporate background, I recommend you consider doing an initial 'scripting' of how you would approach a potential supplier. When you approach them, what do you say – literally – and how do you say it? For example, would you approach a prospective supplier by saying, 'We need someone to provide IT equipment for our staff – what is your record of delivering on time?' Or would you be more likely to say, 'We are looking for a supplier to partner with us for our IT requirements and you come highly recommended. Can we discuss how best we can make use of your service?' Do you see the difference? For most of us on the spectrum, the first example is probably more in line with how we communicate, because that is how we think – direct and to the point. We really aren't into the fluffy bits of the conversation. However, when we are starting a business and establishing business credit for the first time, a bit of fluffiness will go a long way.

It is also worth remembering that in many start-up situations, credit will only be extended to your business with a guarantee from you personally. Do not take this to be offensive, or as a sign that they do not have confidence in your business as a whole. This is just standard business practice for start-ups that as yet do not have any credit rating or history. Usually, the supplier will ask you to complete an application form requesting details of both yourself and your company, and you may well find that you will not be extended credit until you have made an up-front purchase first, using a company debit or credit card. By doing this, the supplier is ensuring that the company is legitimate and the bank account does indeed operate.

Depending on the amount of credit you are looking to obtain, it is also likely that they may well ask you for some financial forecasts for your business. This was covered in Chapter 6, so you should be familiar with the key elements that potential suppliers and banks look at when deciding on your credit potential. I reiterate here that the level of detail required by a supplier is nowhere near the level required by a bank or investor, so make sure that you do not volunteer too much information. While you may see this as being thorough, the potential supplier could see this as a negative and actually use it to reject your application or cap it.

On-going relationships with your suppliers

Once you have been able to establish your supplier accounts, it is very important that you do, in fact, make use of those accounts, even if it is for relatively small amounts. The reason for this is that suppliers monitor their new accounts – especially those of start-ups – to determine activity and potential for future value. If you have been able to obtain an account and then do not use it for six months, this will provide the supplier with an inactivity report, which could very well result in your account being closed. Similarly – and perhaps more obviously – when you start using your account, make certain that you make your monthly payment on time and accurately. During the initial year of trading with the supplier, any delayed payment or underpayment will be severely detrimental to your company's credit record and related credit rating. Of course, making sure your payments are on time should always be a priority but after you have an established account, if for any reason there is a delay in a payment, you can possibly discuss and resolve this with your supplier without an immediate negative reaction from them.

Once you have established a successful and well-managed supplier account for a period in excess of a year, you are then in a position to negotiate better terms on your account if you so wish. This does not mean you will automatically get better terms, but suppliers do generally tend to have more rigid terms for start-ups that relax more as the relationship progresses.

Important considerations for people on the spectrum

There are a couple of points that are important for people on the autism spectrum when it comes to handling suppliers.

The first relates to starting up the supplier account. When you apply for a supplier account, you will – as I have mentioned above – generally be expected to complete and sign an application form, or complete an online application form. Irrespective of the method used, by completing the application form you will be agreeing to the supplier's terms and conditions relating to the account. If you are doing an online application this will generally be more obvious, because they tend to ask you to tick a box saying that you have read, understood and agreed to the terms and conditions of the account. However, a written application can sometimes just make vague mention of the fact that you are agreeing to the terms and conditions by signing the application.

The point I would like to make here is that it is absolutely essential that you do actually read and agree the terms and conditions that are referred to. If the terms and conditions document is not presented to you with the application form, do not sign the application form. Terms and conditions can be extremely binding for you as a new company, and they can also introduce a lot of sharing of your company information with other parties. You could, by signing the application without reading the conditions, inadvertently agree to the supplier sharing your personal and company details with a number of other organisations, or you could be agreeing to be restricted in your trading with competitors, or even committing your company to use the supplier for a minimum period of time with a penalty being charged if you close the account before then.

I do not want to generalise on this point, because as people with ASD we have such varying areas where we find challenges, but if you know that you can sometimes find contracts difficult because you do not always recognise the implicit nuances, or because you get put off by the highly technical nature of some them, I strongly recommend that you get a third party to read the terms and conditions for you. This should be someone you trust, such as a knowledgeable family member, your business advisor or accountant. Make certain you really have read, *understood* and agreed to the terms and conditions before you sign that document.

The second point relates to the on-going supplier relationship. One thing supplier companies are renowned for is their tenacity for getting more business out of new clients. When you set up your account, it is important that you have undertaken the exercise in Chapter 6 to think about what sort of supplies the supplier would be providing you with and how much. The reason for this is because we will often be contacted by the supplier, generally under the guise of seeing how well they are fulfilling our needs. However, in reality these tend to be sales people. So as we start to provide them with feedback (hoping to hear that all has gone well), they then start to advise that there are some additional deals that they think they can offer us, discounts on additional services, and so forth. It is incredibly easy to fall into the trap of taking them up on those offers and deals.

Most of us on the spectrum struggle with the concept of deception – not so much in understanding what it is, but understanding why it is used and that people we are dealing with would want to use deception at all. I have heard it said that most of us on the spectrum are extremely honest people, and as a result we expect others to have the same mind-set. Unfortunately, many don't. We can take their conversations with us to be very genuine, when ultimately the person on the other end of the line has nothing but sales targets in mind and will say whatever they have to in order to raise their sales levels.

If you have taken the time to ensure that you know what your business needs, what the timeframes are for purchasing these and the related budget, it can be far easier to avoid going into over-commitment mode. But keep in mind that sales people are by definition really persistent and persuasive individuals. They can easily convince you that you really do need what they are talking about, even if it is the last thing your business actually does require. For this reason I strongly recommend having a formal supplier communication strategy, and this is quite straightforward. You do not deal with suppliers telephonically. If a supplier calls you and tries to discuss your account, just interrupt them and advise that your company has a formal policy that you do not deal with suppliers telephonically, but that they are more than welcome to submit information to you by post. You will in all likelihood find that the sales person will do their best to continue to speak with you, but you are perfectly entitled to repeat that you do not do business telephonically and politely hang up. If it was a genuine customer service follow-up call, they would respect your initial request for correspondence to be in writing rather than verbal.

Just keep in mind that you are not trying to be rude or too abrupt. You are just being clear with them that you cannot entertain their conversation telephonically but are happy to receive documentation from them. If piles of sales material come through after that, I recommend in your first year that you actually throw this out, since it can be very tempting to purchase more than you have planned to in your initial financial plan. Once your business has been running for at least a year, you are in a position to start looking at additional investments if finances allow.

In summary, ensure that you are aware that you are dealing largely with sales people when being contacted by your supplier, and although you are still building a credit record with them, it is not necessary for you to take on more debt than you intended just because they want to make you spend more.

Chapter 11

Marketing yourself and your Business

Your Public Face

Sometimes one of the most challenging things for Asperger professionals in starting their own businesses is business development. No, not the strategy and planning side of business development – that tends to be something we do very well. Instead, I am talking about that frequently 'nerve-wracking' experience of finding and winning new clients.

Why is it seen as such a challenging experience for so many people on the autism spectrum? Well, hands-on business development requires us to interact with neurotypicals in a way that inspires confidence and makes them want to do business with us. It is one of those times when we feel it is even more important to fit the neurotypical mould. But is it really so important to have our neurotypical mask on when undertaking this critical business activity? Let's discuss this following a look at the experiences of a fellow person on the spectrum.

Case study: Martin's experience of starting up a consultancy

Martin H. (alias) was a well-respected and successful management consultant working in London. His specialisation was in enterprise architecture, and he had worked with some of London's – and even the world's – leading multi-nationals as part of his role within the management consultancy that employed him. Martin had developed a reputation of being able to sell the consultancy and its services to anyone, and indeed a large part of the consultancy's market share had been won by Martin through his passionate selling of the company's abilities, vision and commitment to the client.

After a number of years with the consultancy, Martin began to feel frustrated at not being able to run with his own ideas and passions. He had identified a gap in the consulting market in a specialist area, and had suggested to the consultancy that they start a practice to meet this market need. However, it was seen as outside the consultancy's remit and too much of a diversification, and as a direct consequence Martin took the decision to start his own consultancy, focusing on this specialist field.

Martin was quite confident about the potential for success of his company. He had done his research, knew the specialist field intricately (it was an area of particular interest to him), and he had the contacts within the organisations who would be interested in contracting with him to offer the consultancy. Martin established his business from his own savings, and hired in a couple of administrative people to undertake the business side of the operations, and three junior consultants he intended to train up in his methodologies and vision. His company was established within a month.

Once his company was formalised and things such as a company office, business cards and stationery were ready, Martin started to undertake his business development for his company.

Martin had been confident in his ability to win new business, and therefore did not leave himself too much 'fall-back' funding since he felt it was unnecessary. However, he was surprised to find that his contacts – be they people he had worked with previously or those who knew him by reputation – did not seem to be as motivated by his ideas as his audience always had been when he was selling the services of his employer's consultancy. Most of the meetings, in fact, appeared to leave the potential client uncomfortable or unconvinced about the value of what Martin could offer them. As time went on and no contracts were obtained, Martin began to have doubts about his ability to win business for his consultancy. He knew that the consultants he had hired were far too junior to undertake any business development work, and they were relying on him to provide them with the opportunity to gain experience through some hands-on consulting work. As his confidence in his ability to win business began to wane, so did his self-confidence in respect of his capabilities as a consultant as a whole. This resulted in Martin starting to avoid people, and the cancellation of several business development meetings he had set up.

Within a further two months Martin had completely withdrawn from his new business, resulting in him having to give his staff notice due to lack of funding. Within another month Martin had decided that he was not capable of running his own business, and he dissolved his company and went back into the job market looking for another consultant role, his self-confidence at an all-time low.

The above case study reflects a scenario that is not uncommon, not only for people on the spectrum but for neurotypicals as well. An assumption tends to be made that sales and business development techniques that were successful in the corporate environment will translate naturally into the entrepreneurial environment. In many cases, nothing could be further from the truth. This relates to the concept of you being the face of your business.

Before I start to share some ideas with you about business development and getting sales for your company, we need to discuss the very important topic of marketing and your public face. To clarify what I mean when I talk about your public face: when we start a small business, it is frequently our expertise, knowledge or unique insights that stand to make the business a success. As such, unlike most large corporations, it is our personal reputation that will bring in business. We are the face of the company.

To be fair, there are still large corporations where the leader of the business is the public face of the company. A good example would be Sir Richard Branson. When we see him, we see Virgin. In a similar way, we frequently need to be that visible face representing our new business.

Speaking to some of the entrepreneurs who shared their opinions of entrepreneurship, a number of them indicated that this was something that they currently did, with varying degrees of success. Alex, an entrepreneur from the US, stated: 'My greatest effort in marketing myself as the public face of my business was to create a profile on LinkedIn. The benefits of networking are there but ideal for those shy in a social setting. For me, again, the fear of rejection (or lack of interest!) still sometimes slows me down: in addition, sometimes not knowing how to respond to others' reactions is challenging.'

An entrepreneur from Wales, choosing to remain anonymous, expressed a sentiment shared by many others, saying, '…not as yet, but I will be. I think this will be challenging and terrifying.'

Despite many people finding this similarly challenging, there are also a number of us who have been able to embrace this and are using it effectively, such as Scott Sheinfeld, founder of Infected Sloths LLC. Scott says, 'Yes [*I market my business by being the public face of my company*]. But just market myself, not sales. People know me as a subject matter expert in this field and that's my public face for this business. They know if they come to my business, an expert like me standing [sic] behind it. I even go as far as to serve in board of director positions.' Looking at the more challenging aspects, however, he adds: 'But I am still not sociable. I'd rather not go play in the golfing tournament or appear at more intimate social gatherings. One on one small talk – I can be a potential disaster. So I still have that challenge to overcome.'

Similarly Jeremy Samson, Managing Director of Time2Train shares, 'I am the face of my own business and I enjoy this because I am the final product that each family hope their child will one day grow to be like. I always have made an effort to keep putting myself out there in the spotlight and simply generate more awareness about my program that works naturally. Sometimes a lack of motivation can be a challenge, but I always look for inspiring things to keep on going as well as goal planning and setting.'

It is important to understand how best to represent yourself to your clients in order to optimally market your business.

For those of us coming from a corporate background, this can be quite a significant change in thinking. As professsionals in large businesses, we get used to operating based on the brand of the business that employs us. However, as a small business owner we do not have the authority of the big name, and we need to think about selling ourselves rather than trying to sell an unknown small business name.

Related to this is the challenge for some of us of having to ensure that the face we present to the public is appealing and motivating. Sometimes this can be hard. Let's think of an example. Josh is an individual on the autism spectrum. He generally struggles with things such as making eye contact and speaking with people (having a soft voice he struggles to project) and he is hypersensitive to light. As a result he frequently ends up either wearing sunglasses all the time, or squinting against the light. His family have shared with him that he has a tendency to frown, but it isn't something he has taken particular notice of.

In starting his own business, his attempts to become the face of his company were very challenging. First of all, neurotypical people tend to struggle to trust individuals who do not make eye contact. Add to that someone who is constantly frowning and squinting, and mumbling rather than speaking, and we do not really have a good public face.

Developing an appropriate public face does not always necessarily mean that you cannot reflect those unique characteristics that are you. I very strongly disagree with those who say that if a person is to be a successful advocate for their business they need to fit the almost stereotypical charismatic extrovert personality type. I also disagree with those who say that all differences you have should be suppressed. I don't know about you, but I am proud of who I am and I do not intend to pretend to be someone I am not. However, I do agree that sometimes we need to be aware of the areas that could be challenging for neurotypicals to accept, understand or feel comfortable with, and find a strategy for dealing with that.

Here are some key considerations for you in thinking about your public face.

If you're different, you will stand out from the crowd

In being the face of your business, it is good to know that being different will make you stand out from the crowd. However, you would obviously prefer to stand out from the crowd in a positive way rather than a negative way. When you are thinking about branding your business, keep in mind some of the unique characteristics that you are bringing to it that will add value, and see if you can find a way to incorporate that uniqueness. Sometimes it can be in the actual logo you use; sometimes it is in the company name or descriptor. For example, if we have a look at the branding for Asperger Leaders, an organisation I chair that mentors and develops people on the autism spectrum holding leadership positions in business, we emphasise our uniqueness as part of the company name and descriptor, namely 'leadership from a unique perspective'.

Be aware of how you present visually

You are going to be representing your business to potential clients, suppliers and investors. How do you appear when you present to them? Are you coming across as arrogant, shy, unconfident, overbearing? I always recommend that people get the advice of someone whom they trust, or that they perhaps record a movie of themselves making a pitch presentation to review afterwards. Another option is to just watch yourself in the mirror as you are making a presentation. Ideally, however, it is always a good idea to get the feedback of a neurotypical, because they will be watching you from a different perspective.

Don't conform, but don't alienate

When it comes to things such as how you dress to undertake a presentation to a potential client and so forth, we do need to consider how we dress and our overall outward face. While – as I have said already – I do not agree that people need to conform to other people's standards as part of their transition to an entrepreneur, I do believe it is important that you do not alienate your potential clients. What I am saying is that you should emphasise your distinctive 'you' while not over emphasising your differences.

You are ultimately selling yourself, not a corporate brand

As mentioned earlier, one of the changes in mind-set between selling as part of your corporate career and selling on behalf of your own business is that in the latter case you are effectively selling you rather than a company name. You are the person who can make the sale by being knowledgeable, passionate and genuine.

Chapter 12

Initial Business Development

So often, we start our businesses because we know very well what we are offering and the value it will bring to the market. However, when we think about how to go about finding actual customers or clients to benefit from that product or service, we come up short. Business development in itself can be an area of incredible stress for people on the spectrum, not only because it is generally very face-to-face, but largely because it relates to selling a service or product to others and negotiating on terms and fees. It is generally fair to say that most people on the spectrum do not make very good sales people for two reasons:

- We tend to be very honest people, and if we think a customer could get a better deal somewhere else we'll tell them so.

- Negotiation tends not to be a strong point, so we will either agree to offer something (including our own services) below the optimal price, or we will end up alienating customers by refusing to budget on prices.

So what are some of the most important things we need to keep in mind as we start to develop our new business?

The first steps – before you start business development...

There are a number of things you should ensure you do before you start to actively go looking for new business.

Know what you are offering and its appeal to others

Those of us with an autism spectrum disorder often have a far more intrinsic understanding of the value of our product than most people. We can see how products can be used, services applied, value created. We understand it – but we need to make sure that we are able to communicate that value to other people in a way that will appeal to them.

If we are selling a product, this tends to be easier. Make a list of the unique features and value of the product, and then try to imagine how each of these positives could appeal to an individual (or company) buying the product. Think of examples, including how the purchaser would be satisfied and exactly why. Do your best to think of as many different types of buyers as possible, and as many reasons for them being pleased as possible. The reason for this is to prepare you for having discussions with potential clients. As you meet with people, they may ask you questions about how your product could be a benefit in certain situations. If you have prepared yourself for this, you will be able to accurately and concisely describe the added value of your product and come across as knowledgeable and confident.

If you are selling a service, such as business services or consultancy, a large part of knowing what you are offering is understanding what it is that you can offer to your client, what makes your service valuable, the benefits to their business, your competence and/or expertise in the area concerned. Make certain that you are able to call to mind recent examples of the work you have done in other companies, with a focus on the value you have added to their business, such as cost savings, increased productivity, and so forth. Again, take the time to try to put yourself into your potential client's shoes in order to explain how best you could support them and bring benefits to the business. Understanding how neurotypicals are motivated and respond can sometimes be challenging for people with Asperger's. If this is you, I suggest that you perhaps try to get some input on your thinking from other neurotypicals, such as family or friends.

It is generally not appropriate to mention the names of your other clients unless you have their permission to do so, therefore you need to ensure that previous clients are happy for you to use them as a reference.

Know your potential customer

This sounds obvious, but again this comes back to understanding the neurotypical mind in some ways. For example, what is your typical customer likely to find appealing? What will they find unappealing? What will make them consider your services over others? Other questions include: What industry are they likely to be in? What level are they likely to be in the organisation – do you need to sell to staff, to managers or to directors?

Know your competition

Ensure that you are aware of your competitors in the marketplace and what their unique selling points are. What makes their offering different to yours? What makes yours a better offer than theirs? In what way can you match their services, and in what ways can you outdo them? In addition, be honest about areas where you cannot match what they offer, but ensure that you can offer something else instead. Make sure that you commit all of this to memory so that if a potential customer asks you questions, you can answer confidently and knowledgeably.

Make sure you know and accurately share your professional image (branding)

Branding when you are a service provider is extremely important. Potential clients get to see you through the public face of your marketing and branding, as discussed in the previous chapter. Before they make the decision to work with you, they will look at your branding – who are you professing to be? Are you projecting yourself as an international specialist or consultant in a unique field? Are you projecting the image of a down-to-earth, roll-up the sleeves consultant? What do you want to reflect? What does your business need you to reflect? Make sure that your branding reflects that you are a confident professional, but not an arrogant know-it-all. Once you have done that, make sure that you have business cards, letterheads and other stationery that is in line with your branding – and always ensure that you have business cards with you!

Some essential tips for Asperger professionals in finding new business

As mentioned above, there are really two forms of business development: business development when you have a physical product, and business development when you are selling services of some kind. What follows relates largely to winning new business when you are selling some sort of service.

Undertake direct marketing

Direct marketing can be a two-edged sword. Many executives are flooded with direct marketing every day and can get very negative towards it. However, unless you get your details out there, you could very well lose a business opportunity purely due to the fact that you are unknown to your potential clients. The best thing to do is to develop a very focused, creative and appealing flyer that you can send through to your identified potential business clients. Possibly add some sort of incentive for them to want to read it – such as a discount on services within a certain period, or linking the services to an upcoming seminar, event or change in government regulatory requirements that may affect them. Personally, I do not recommend email marketing unless you have been invited to contact the particular potential client by email.

Start a specialist blog

If you are offering services in a very specific area, you may want to think about starting a specialist blog. This is a very good option for people with Asperger's, since it allows us to show our knowledge in an area and build a presence without the need for face-to-face networking to the same degree. There are a few things to consider in doing this, however. First, you do need to ensure that you keep it updated regularly. You need to share valuable information with readers – enough that shows you know your stuff and are an expert, but not so much that readers will ultimately no longer need your services. Make sure subscribers to your blog give their consent to receive additional information from you, and then make use of your direct marketing information to send them offers and updates. You also need to ensure that your blog has sufficient visibility for your potential clients – research where you can make your blog known, or consider advertising somewhere.

Contribute to other online forums

Once again, this is a useful business development tool for those of us on the spectrum. Make certain that you are aware of some key industry forums, or forums which may attract readers who are likely to be potential clients for your own business. Build a presence on the forums by making valuable contributions and comments. I do not recommend that you try to sell your business via other forums, but rather that you get your name out there. In describing yourself, you would mention the name of your business (for example, Consultant: Asperger Leaders), but do not put any marketing content in your comments or articles. You are building awareness, not selling.

Write articles for hard copy and online magazines or journals

Be proactive in developing a set of articles that you can contribute to various magazines or journals. Writing – whether this is online or in hard-copy magazines – is an excellent way to get your name and the name of your organisation into public sight. Remember, potential clients frequently find their service providers by doing internet searches. You need your name and company name to come up when they do so. Unlike contributing to forums, it is acceptable to add a paragraph at the end of your article describing your company and your role within it, together with a sentence or two about what you offer.

Get in the news

Of course, one of the best ways to build awareness of yourself or your company is to do something newsworthy and then do a press release. This may be harder to do, but the nice thing about a press release is that you often do not need to actually speak to the journalist, but can just correspond in writing. Be prepared, however, for one of them to invite you to be interviewed. Ensure that you have prepared a number of generic responses and have committed them to memory. This will help avoid you suffering a mind blank when you are potentially being overloaded in an interview situation.

Build partnerships with other businesses

Another thing that can be helpful is building partnerships with other companies that are in a related area but not competition. For example, if you are providing complementary services, you could get them to recommend you, and you could recommend them. Or you could agree that if they take on a contract, they have you as a preferred subcontractor and vice versa.

Still the most essential part – networking

Like it or not, the most important part of business development is actually networking. Many people with ASD shrink visibly at the thought of networking – it just isn't natural for us. Nevertheless, it is an essential component in building new business. Given the essential nature of networking, I have covered this in more detail in Chapter 15.

Be aware of how you present yourself

This has already been discussed in an earlier chapter, but it is always important to understand how other people see or perceive you. If you are doing face-to-face selling, make sure that you have had feedback on how you present when selling, when closing a sale and when asking about new opportunities – in other words when prospecting.

Negotiation

Negotiation is an essential part of business development. No matter how good we know or believe our product to be, it is important to recognise that we will generally be expected to negotiate terms with a new client. This could be a negotiation in terms of price, but it could also be in terms of things like a guarantee, additional support or extra consultancy hours. It is a good plan to have a formal cut-off line for your negotiations determined in your organisation before you go into the meeting. That way you know the most you can reduce your costs to in order to still make a profit. It is also good practice to initially charge marginally more for your product or service than your straight profit amount, since this allows you to have a bit more flexibility to lower prices.

When you have negotiated to the point where you would be suffering a loss if you went any further, make certain that you communicate to the client that this really is the cut-off point and that you are unable to go beyond this. You need to be firm at this point and not be tempted to offer any more discounts. Not only will this be detrimental to your business revenues, but giving in further at this point could lose you credibility with the new client.

Confirming your sale

It is very important that you get written confirmation of a sale as soon as you can. If you do not have standard sales forms (for example, if you are selling a service rather than a product), then it is important that you send a formal contract as soon as you can have it drawn up. However, it is good practice to send an email confirmation of the sale as soon as you can after the meeting, confirming that a contract will be forwarded and thanking them for their business.

Follow-up

It is very good practice for you to follow up with your new clients or customers. Send them an email to see if they are happy with the product or service, or ideally give them a call. This should be done two to three weeks after their purchase, which gives them time to use their product/service before giving feedback. Remember to be open to feedback at that time.

Don't take a non-sale personally

There are going to be many times when you are not successful in your bid for business with a client – that is the nature of business. It is very tempting for people – especially those of us on the spectrum – to be tempted to take the failure to secure a sale as a personal failure and a form of rejection. Remember, this is business – it is not about you as an individual. The client could think you and your product are absolutely the best thing since sliced bread, but just not have the budget for what you are offering for the next 12 months. It has nothing to do with you. However, it is always good to ask for feedback on why the potential client is not going with the sale. Sometimes you may be surprised to hear from them that there was a concern about your presentation, or some of the material you used for the presentation to them. If you are aware of this, you can review it for your next business development meeting.

Business development and the related sales process can be challenging, but it is also highly rewarding when you win that first contract. If this is an area in which you particularly struggle, you may want to consider whether it is worthwhile investing in a business development person. Just be sure that if you do this, you make time to train them up in your expected standards, ethics and morals so that they know exactly how they should be selling to your potential clients and what they should and shouldn't be doing as part of their business development client negotiations.

Chapter 13

The Tender and Contracting Process

In many business sectors, the accepted manner for organisations to win business is through a formal tender process. Generally, this tends to be for contracts of significant value, but they can also be used by organisations in specific business sectors (for example public sector or not-for-profit) or as a requirement for a transparent piece of work (for example, undertaking a consultancy programme where appointment of the consultancy needs to be demonstrably fair and unbiased, due to public documentation or trade union requirements).

For many people on the spectrum, the formality of the tender and contracting process can be very off-putting when thinking about starting a business, since it is all about selling ourselves and our product, and is intricately linked to how we present ourselves. However, I am confident that by now you have already done some work in respect of how you present yourself to potential customers, as well as on developing a unique brand or identity for your company. This will help significantly in raising your level of confidence with respect to handling a tender presentation and potentially winning the contract. Additionally, the information in this chapter should provide some insights into the process and what you need to do to ensure you have the best chance of success in your bid.

There are few things that I am going to cover in this chapter, starting with clarification of what the usual tender and contracting process involves, followed by some recommendations in respect of best practice for tenders, as well as some recommendations specifically relating to some of the areas where we may be challenged.

Let us start by examining the tender and contracting process in a little more detail for those people who have never been involved in a tender process.

What is the tender and contracting process?

A tender process is where an organisation advises external providers in the marketplace of a particular business need or requirement they have and formally invites them to tender (or bid) for the business or express an interest in undertaking the work. This effectively allows a wide number of potential suppliers to compete for the business.

The process formally starts with the organisation in need of a service pulling together a tender document. This can be called different things depending on the country and business sector you are in, but generally is one of the following:

- Invitation to Tender (ITT)

- Invitation to Bid (BTI)

- Request for Proposal (RFP)

- Request for Tender (RFT).

For ease of reference, I will refer to this documentation as the invitation to tender going forward. Irrespective of what it is called, this document will contain a very detailed breakdown of the need of the organisation or issue that needs addressing, as well as any particular requirements, submission criteria, restrictions or specific instructions for response. If you want to tender for this contract, you then prepare a formal tender bid document. The invitation to tender documentation will generally be specific about the format of this proposal, but sometimes they leave this to the tendering company to determine in order to establish how good the tendering company is at developing documentation and proposals without formal direction.

Whatever the specific format of the tender bid requested by the organisation, there are some essentials that need to be included in your document, and these are the pricing of your work, any schedules or proposed first level project plans, and a summary of how you feel you meet the specified criteria of the tender request document. Later in the chapter I will speak about what other things can be added to your tender bid document to make this more effective.

Once tender bids have been submitted and the closing date for the tender process reached, the tender bids will be evaluated. This tends to be a very formal and structured process that you would have been made aware of as part of the invitation to tender documentation. It tends to involve scoring the tender bids against a number of specified criteria according to a transparent scoring system, and frequently with a formal weighting system as well. Later on in the chapter I will make reference to some examples of what these documents can look like.

Once the successful provider has been selected, they are then formally advised they have been successful, and the unsuccessful tendering companies advised they have not been successful. Depending on your country and the type of tender contract that is being offered, this is frequently followed by a formal holding period, where the other tenderers have the opportunity to appeal the decision if they feel that assessment has not been in line with the documented evaluation criteria. Once that holding period has finished, a contract will be formally awarded and the work can start.

The practicalities of operating within the tender market

Perhaps one of the first things for me to cover initially relates to your actual suitability to tender for the work. When you make the decision to start a business that is going to get a large part of its business revenue through the tender process, it is important to keep in mind that you are likely to experience challenges in this area in the first few years of your business trading. This is because tender evaluations generally look at how long the tendering company has been in business, as well as such things as similar work undertaken by the business, and the size and type of clients they have had or currently have. If you are a start-up, any references to experience and clients would only come from your previous working career – if at all. Therefore, it is advisable to try to win some business for your company outside the tender process ahead of making the decision to move into the tender market so you will be able to provide clients' references when making any tenders in the future.

That isn't to say that you may not be able to win some contracts if yours is a very niche area and where your reputation as a specialist in the corporate world holds weight. However, this tends to be more of the exception rather than the rule due to the formal and rigid format of the assessment criteria used in the evaluation process.

Developing your tender bid

Now that we know what the tender and contracting process involves, let us have a look in a bit more detail at some of the elements of developing a potentially successful tender proposition.

Reviewing the tender document

The first step in the tender process is for you to actually have a look at the organisation's invitation to tender document. In Toolkit Exercise 7 in Part 5 of the book, you will find an example of an invitation to tender document. Although the format of such documents can vary considerably, the general outline tends to be very similar. I recommend that you review this template now, and return to your reading here once you have done so.

The first thing to do in reviewing your invitation to tender is to have a detailed read of the document and identify exactly what it is the client needs done. Ensure that you go through any criteria that they list and confirm that you are able to meet their needs in this respect. If there are any criteria you do not meet – stop. Do not try to build a case that says, effectively, that you do not meet all the requirements for the tender but can make up for it by doing x, y, or z. Procurement teams have very strict evaluation rules, and if you do not match all the required criteria listed, you will automatically be rejected. In fact, all it does do is annoy procurement teams who have to read through proposals that end up being 'outside of scope', thereby wasting their time. Should a further tender come up, you could already have earned yourself a bad reputation had you done that.

If you are confident that the tender request covers an area of service that you can address, your next step is to consider the size of the project. Have a detailed look at what they are asking for and what they are likely to expect from you in terms of time commitments. Are you able to resource the project appropriately? Do you have enough people at a senior enough level to handle the work requirements and satisfy any evaluation criteria regarding your human resources? Are you certain that there are no other project commitments that could impinge on your commitments to this new project at any key milestone dates? These are some of the sorts of questions you need to ask yourself before you even think of pulling together a formal bid. The company posting the tender deserves nothing less than 100 per cent on their project – are you certain that you are able to offer that?

I would also invite you, as a person on the autism spectrum, to consider a couple of additional questions in respect of the tender work. First, if you are going to be the lead consultant in the work, are there likely to be any areas that could be challenging for you in terms of either people skills or communication? What do I mean by this? Well, as an example, if you were going to put in a tender bid for the development and implementation of a new performance management system in a business, have you checked whether the client is expecting you to undertake staff training on the system as part of the remit, or be involved in the negotiation of its introduction with the trade union? Do you think this is something you would be able to handle confidently, or is your skill on the technical and implementation side?

By now, I am sure that you are relatively familiar with elements of dealing with neurotypicals that you find challenging. It is important that, in looking to take on a tender proposal, you consider anything that may be challenging for you as far as people skills is concerned, and then consider your options in that respect. For example, in the example give above, you could split the lead on the project work between yourself and another member of your company, so that you do the development and implementation and he or she does the training. Whatever your decision regarding whether or not to undertake the work, make certain that you do consider your own strengths and limitations as part of your review.

I also suggest that you consider if there is any potential for challenges in respect of sensitivities. If you have hyper- or hyposensitivity issues, you need to re-read the tender criteria and background information to determine whether there are any implications for you in this area. If the tender proposal is to undertake some contracting work on an industrial site, but you have hypersensitive hearing, this is going to be a problem for you. Similarly, if the project involves working in a highly crowded environment, this can sometimes also be a challenge.

Above all else, make certain that you consider these sorts of things. As I said previously, your client deserves nothing less than the best and if such things as sensory overloads are hindering your performance, this is not fair to your client. I am not saying that you cannot undertake the work if you suffer from sensory overload. What I am saying is that you need to identify any potential issues, assess whether they are manageable and make an honest decision in respect of whether this will interfere with the project or not. If they will, and it is essential that you do the work rather than someone else in your team, give this particular tender a miss.

Researching the client

Another key element of reviewing the tender is to actually do some additional work researching the client. In order for you to understand how best to meet the needs of the client, you need to have some insights into what is considered important for them. If you are submitting a tender, is the most important element for the client going to be the cost effectiveness of your quote, or is quality their key focus? Do they have a reputation for working with companies that are openly transparent and diverse, or is the reputation of the supplier in the marketplace the most important consideration?

Have a look at some historical information on the company concerned. Are they in a growth stage, or are they consolidating? Have they recently been through an organisational restructure or a merger? This can tell you a lot about what would be important for them, and can be useful for you in pulling together your tender.

Writing your proposal

This is one of the most important parts of the process, since the proposal you send through will determine whether or not you reach the next stage of the process. The format of your tender document will largely be determined by what the potential client has asked for in their invitation to tender. They will have detailed some very specific evaluation criteria, and it is generally very useful for the client if you pull together a table towards the beginning of your tender which shows where the information addressing those requirement can be found in the document. Note that this is not the same as the index, since your tender will contain more information than this, but is rather something the customer can use as they read your document to move easily between areas they wish to assess.

Some of the key considerations you need to take into account are the following:

- Make certain that you respond to each and every evaluation criteria area identified by the customer in the tender document. Ensure that the responses you provide are not ambiguous in any way or unclear.

- Make certain that the document reflects your prior experience in the areas concerned without appearing to be arrogant. I have seen so many service providers lose a tender because of sweeping statements like 'we are the best in the market' and 'signing with us means you will never again experience any problems'. Be confident but not overwhelming. It would be better to say things like, 'Our clients have advised us we have provided the best service they have ever had' and so on.

- Make sure your tender is not only cost effective but also value-adding. Depending on the customer, weightings for cost and value can vary significantly.

- Try to get someone to read it to check for grammar, spelling and consistency. Sometimes we can get so close to a document that we overlook these.

- Make sure you submit your proposal with plenty of time to spare.

Attending an evaluation meeting

Some invitations to tender require that shortlisted bidders give a presentation to an evaluation panel as part of the final assessment. If this is the case, there are a few suggestions I would make to you in attending this meeting.

- Make certain that your presentation is not too long or too short. If you are uncertain of the length of time you have with the client, you should contact them through the accepted channel and ask for this information. Customers want you to get to the point, and not spend too much time on history, who you are, etc.

- Make certain that the standard of your presentation is acceptable. If you are not familiar with such software as PowerPoint and the related graphics and animations, get someone to help you. A good presentation indicates to the customer that you are professional and that you care about presenting your best to them.

- Ensure that any equipment you are going to use is working properly and that the customer has the technical requirements needed: for example, do you need to connect to their overhead or should you bring your own?

- Dress the part. I know that this can sometimes be a challenging area for some of us who have sensitivities, but it really is an important point. Customers will judge you on your appearance, like it or not. They can be very impressed by your proposal, but totally put off by how you have presented yourself. I recently attended a tender evaluation meeting to support a client choosing a new consultancy. Prior to the presentations, one particular consultancy had made a significant impression on the team. Their initial marking against some of the paper-based evaluation criteria indicated that they were likely to be successful – that is, until they walked in the room. The lead consultant was dressed in business trousers, a shirt with no tie, and tweed jacket. His hair was untidy and he was wearing what can best be described as loafer shoes. His female associate was wearing a smart business skirt suit and was well presented. However, the evaluation team was visibly shocked at the lack of decorum of the lead consultant in turning up to an evaluation meeting in anything less than a formal business suit. Needless to say, despite the appropriate presentation of the second consultant, the tender was lost due to the lack of business attire on the part of the lead consultant.

- Present yourself correctly. Apart from how you dress, make sure that your hair and make-up (if appropriate) are smart. Also, when you go into the meeting make sure that you smile, introduce yourself and offer to shake hands (if you can – sometimes there can be a horseshoe type presentation room where you cannot get to the evaluator panel). Start your presentation promptly. Make sure that you speak confidently but not too loudly. I recommend that ahead of your presentation you actually practise this with someone with a business background so that you can get an idea of how your speaking voice comes across. You may have to practise increasing your volume or decreasing your volume. Also be aware that you do not want to speak too fast. While it is also not really ideal to speak too slowly, it is better to speak slower than to speak too fast. Make sure that you speak clearly.

- Think about your body language when you present. What are you doing with your hands when you present? How are you standing? If you are standing, are you standing straight or are you slouching? I must admit that when I start a presentation with a prospective client, I am very aware of the fact that if I sit down and present I can start stimming, and if I am standing in one spot I end up moving from one foot to the other, which doesn't give a good impression. Therefore, I always start by saying to the client that I hope they don't mind it, but I tend to move around a little when making a presentation – too much energy to stand in one spot. Most people will not have a problem with that and will generally smile at the joke. Find a way in advance to deal with any particular points you feel you may need to consider.

- When people in the panel ask you questions, beware of frowning. I know it can be very easy to do this when listening to a speaker, but this can give a very negative impression to the person asking the question. Instead make eye contact, and nod occasionally to indicate that you are following them. When answering the question, make your response direct and to the point, but not a one-word answer.

- Beware of being defensive. Many evaluators will deliberately try to 'pick holes' in your presentation and proposal to see how you respond. If you respond defensively and aggressively, you will have lost the tender. Instead, try to prepare for the meeting with a coping strategy. For example, my coping strategy is that if a person in an evaluation panel asks me a question that makes me feel insulted, undermined, angry or otherwise compromised, I ensure that before I reply I visualise that person's comment as a bubble in my head, and I mentally reach up and put it in a box, together with my visualised reactions. I have learnt to do this very rapidly, since evaluators are not going to wait for you to do this in your head for two minutes before responding. Therefore, if you are prone to reacting strongly to criticism, I suggest you practise doing this with someone you know and trust who can make negative comments to you and you can practise handling them. Another technique is to just visualise something like patting the person on the head before you answer, or laughing in their face. But whatever your coping strategy ultimately ends up being, make certain that you always keep in mind that in all likelihood the person does not really mean any negative comments they may be making, but are seeking to test you. Make sure you pass the test.

- When the session is finished, thank the panel and then leave punctually.

- If you are the sort of business that will be doing a lot of tendering, I would strongly recommend that you take some time to read one of the many books on the market that go into detail about the tendering process and specific requirements for tender documents, such as *Bids, Tenders and Proposals* (Lewis 2012) or *Basics Tendering* (Brandt 2007).

PART 4

Personal Development for Entrepreneurs on the Autism Spectrum

Chapter 14

Developing Working Relationships

Once again, people who have made the move from corporate leadership roles into more entrepreneurial positions will find that their working relationships are likely to change significantly. As a professional in the larger business world, you would have developed managerial and leadership skills appropriate to larger organisations, taking into account such things as formalised performance appraisal systems, time management systems, management information from a human resources information system, and so forth. You will be used to holding regular meetings with your direct reports, who will update you on their teams' performance. It is likely that you would have relatively irregular meetings with the entire workforce, if any.

But now you are in your own company, where the scale of employees is vastly different (in all probability), and where it is necessary for most people to report to you directly. Some people moving from corporate roles to their own companies get tied up in trying to replicate the human resources systems that they have worked with in their previous companies, mirroring everything from organisational charts to time-management systems. However, there are very few small companies that operate optimally with such an elaborate employee framework, working best with far flatter organisational structures and less rigid time and policy constraints.

This means that, whereas in your area of the business in your corporate job you may have had a number of managers reporting to you who were ultimately responsible for the staff, now you may be the only real manager in the company. As a result, the way you communicate with people is going to change and in all likelihood the level of formality is going to decrease. Whereas you may have previously have had formal meetings which have been regularly scheduled, attended and minuted, now discussions are likely to be more informal and all inclusive and – with the exception of key strategic or operational meetings – these really would not be minuted in the same way.

One of the greatest attractions for people working in small companies tends to be the less rigid and formal environment. Many creative and talented people (including yourself) have taken the decision to sacrifice job security and a steady pay cheque for the independence and 'buzz' employment within a small company can offer them. This may seem an obvious statement, but it is an important thing to keep in mind when you consider how to establish your working environment and the relationships therein. Replicating the formal, rigid, structured systems of the corporation will do nothing other than drive your entrepreneur away from your business, no matter how good the opportunity or how competitive the pay.

One of the things I have learnt over the years is that many of us with Asperger's can find it challenging to put others into our shoes. What do I mean by this? Well, it is a relatively well-known characteristic that we have what is known as 'mind-blindness' (Baron-Cohen 1997) or what Tony Attwood calls 'impaired theory of mind' (Attwood 2007). According to Attwood, this refers to a weakness in 'the ability to recognize and understand thoughts, beliefs, desires and intentions of other people in order to make sense of their behavior and predict what they are going to do next' (p.112). But I would add to this the situation where we experience something and understand how it affects us, but struggle to see other people having the same experience.

So, as an example, while we recognise and understand the intense feelings we have had to become independent and start our own businesses, we may not always identify that the people who come into our companies out of the corporate world have probably gone through exactly the same revelation. They, too, have felt stifled and constrained, and longed to be more creative, having the freedom and independence to give it their all without the red tape and politics. How, then, do you think they would feel if we start to introduce red tape and overly formal systems into the small company they have joined? Perhaps what you should do is ask yourself this question instead: 'If I started my own company, how would I feel if someone outside the company suddenly started to introduce rules, red tape and formality that I believed was interfering with my independence and creativity?'

When you have considered this question, and embraced how you would experience this personally, you need to now recognise that these feelings are likely to be the same ones your employees would be experiencing if you started to develop an overly formal structure in your small company. Perhaps this will help you consider the impact of your actions, and to possibly modify them. In any event, it may help if you have been finding that some of your previously enthusiastic staff appear suddenly negative or demotivated – are you trying to turn your entrepreneurial business into a corporate?

So let us return to the topic of working relationships. As I mentioned above, it is highly likely that you will now have a number of people of different levels of responsibility reporting in to you. Depending on the size of your business, this may actually be the entire workforce. If you have a business with ten employees, for example, it is going to be expected that you provide their direction and guidance. It is not really viable to have managers acting on your behalf (although you may well have some sort of supervisor for times you are not available). Therefore, it is important that you develop appropriate working relationships with your team. Again, as mentioned above, informality and collegiate working are frequently very important elements in the motivation of a small work team, but there is a fine line between being informal and being pally or friends. You are still working colleagues and you need to keep your relationships professional. But you also need to make sure that you are open enough to your teams to allow them to talk freely with you and feel confident enough to come to you with ideas or concerns about the business.

So how do we get that balance right? How do we know when we are being informal or formal enough, or whether or not we have become too personal versus too professional? There isn't a straightforward answer to that question, since there are a couple of dependencies here. The answer depends on the nature of your business and the sector in which you are operating (since this is likely to have a direct effect on your business's culture), how you know your colleagues (did you all come across from the corporate employer you have left, or are they staff you recruited?), and just how many people there are in the business. Irrespective of answers to the above questions, I can offer you some general guidance to help you with the basics.

Get to know your team

This may seem like an obvious point, but you will be surprised at the number of people on the spectrum who can overlook this requirement – and large number of neurotypicals as well! When I say that you need to get to know your team, I mean that you need to know people's names and what they do in the company – where have they come from and where to they want to grow to. Dependent on the number of people in your business, you cannot be expected to know a lot of details about everyone, but what is important is that you make the effort and be seen to take an interest in your people.

Greet your team

This is another Asperger's issue for some people. Often, we will come into work in the morning and start talking business with our teams, perhaps even mentioning successes in the previous day or week, and so forth. However, have you actually taken the time to greet them informally during the course of the morning? Again, depending on the size of your business, you aren't expected to walk around the company in the morning saying hello to everyone. However, making contact in some form or another is important – say good morning to your receptionist, ask your web designer if he had a good evening, don't be averse to offering to make a cup of coffee for someone else.

Let your team get to know you

Even those of us who are particularly good at people skills in general may very well face a challenge when it comes to actually sharing details of your own personal life with others. Those of us with Asperger's tend to be pretty guarded about sharing this sort of information in the workplace, generally because we may feel this puts us at risk of exposing any communication or social shortcomings. However, this can be very important in the more informal and collegiate environment of the small business world. Once again, let us consider the degree to which it is important to be open with your employees and colleagues.

Sometimes new entrepreneurs will discover that after they have recruited their key people for their business and put what they believe to be appropriate structures in place, new employees who were initially excited and motivated appear to start losing some of that enthusiasm. Let's look at a case study to make what I am talking about clearer.

Case study: Denise's virtual office – An example of entrepreneurial people challenges

Denise was a highly successful office manager within a medium-sized organisation based in South Africa. Although she had not intended to become an office manager, her earlier work ambitions had been stifled by challenges she had experienced in the workplace as a direct result of her autism, albeit that she had been diagnosed with Asperger's early enough to develop reasonable coping strategies. Denise had always wanted to be in human resources, but she found that this did not reflect her strengths and she knew if she stayed in this function she would never progress as far as she wanted. Therefore, when the opportunity arose she applied for the position internally and was appointed on a probationary trial. She had never looked back, and neither had the company.

After five years in the role – the longest she had ever held one position – Denise started to think about opportunities to start an independent business. Despite the job she was doing being far more suited to her strengths, she still felt she had so much more to offer, and felt stifled by the rules and regulations of the medium-sized corporation she was employed by. Creativity or any kind of entrepreneurship was discouraged, being seen as the sole remit of the executive team, and her ideas for improved productivity and new revenue streams for the business never seemed to be taken very seriously, Denise often feeling as if her line manager was 'patting her on the head' rather than taking her suggestions seriously.

One of the suggestions Denise had put forward was the concept of virtual offices. One of the company's services was small business support, and therefore Denise had researched where gaps existed in the market for this population, and the most predominant was the area of affordable office space and business support. Many small business owners or independent consultants did not need physical office space, but just a registered office address, telephone number and someone to take the calls. Others also required the ad hoc services of personal assistants and book-keepers, not having the amount of work required to justify the salaries of even part-time staff. There were also small businesses working in remote locations where it was unlikely that they would be able to find professional staff who would be willing to relocate or commute to such out of the way (and potentially dangerous) locations. Denise had drawn up a business model of a cost-effective virtual office and on demand PA (personal assistant) and book-keeper service, which she had tested anonymously in the marketplace with great results. It was obviously something small business owners in South Africa were very eager to take advantage of.

When Denise received the usual rebuff from her line manager, she made the decision to resign from her company and start up a business of her own, which she went ahead and did. She was well aware of the fact that many of the personal assistants and book-keepers working within her company (and those she had spoken with as part of her research) were frustrated with working within the corporate machine and longed to be able to work from home or at least more flexibly. Denise took advantage of this, setting up her virtual office to have a physical office (for the purposes of offering a registered address to clients), but restricting the use of this largely to providing meeting rooms for clients and having a reception. The rest of the support staff (PAs, book-keepers and payroll administrators) worked from their own homes on a flexible shift basis. The model appeared to be ideal for the staff and for the new clients.

Denise was determined to make her small business a professional one. For this reason she determined that it would be best if she set up a formal shift system rather than making the shifts more flexible, because she was concerned that having too much flexibility would result in insufficient cover and possibly lowered customer service. She communicated this to her team and advised them about a new time-logging portal she had established and told them to start using it. She also advised the team that there would be weekly team meetings held via teleconference, at a time that would overlap between the two shifts. This meant that on this day people on the two shifts had to work a little longer than usual. Attendance was compulsory.

At the first team meeting, Denise received some feedback from one of her team, who asked if the issue of flexibility could be reconsidered. Denise advised them that this was the way the company was going to run because it was necessary in order for it to be professional. Another member of her team started to make a suggestion about how else this could work, but Denise interrupted her to advise that the purpose of the meeting was to discuss work, not for them to try to do her job for her.

As the months went by, Denise started to notice that her once enthusiastic team were becoming more and more demotivated and even negative. She tried to address this by introducing an incentive scheme for them that paid them for positive feedback from clients, but if anything this had the opposite effect, since clients were actually starting to complain about the lack of commitment from the team.

Denise was totally confused as to what was going on. Why were her staff being so negative?

Denise had made the first mistake of moving from the corporate to entrepreneurial setting – she had carried the corporate mind-set with her. By introducing a shift system and formal team meeting system, she had inadvertently brought into her company all of the things her staff were trying to get away from. The people joining her were individuals who wanted the flexibility of working from home under less constrained conditions. Denise's new system effectively removed this opportunity from them, and it is likely that the staff ended up feeling taken advantage of and misled.

One of the frustrations that Denise had experienced was that she had never been allowed to have an input into her company, despite knowing very well that her contributions would have been valuable. However, in running her business, she had actually imposed the same uncomfortable restriction onto her own staff. When they had tried to make suggestions in the team meeting, they were told in no uncertain terms that decision making was her responsibility, not theirs. She had blocked them from making any contribution in the future by implying that any comment from them indicated that they were questioning her judgement.

In talking Denise through the situation, she was asked to consider a different company where she had gone to work as a virtual assistant, and I asked her to comment on how she would have felt if the same restrictions she had created were introduced into her new company soon after she had joined. Denise recognised that she would have been annoyed, and that she would have been particularly unreceptive to the lack of ability to make a contribution, having experienced that recently. Putting this into context, Denise was rather shocked to realise that this was exactly what she had done in her own company.

Try to reverse the roles

Developing working relationships is never easy. However, in order to ensure that you do not create bad feelings unintentionally, I strongly recommend a technique (described above) that a psychologist I work with introduced me to. This is where you try to imagine what the other person is feeling by describing a similar situation where you are the person experiencing whatever is going on.

I know that as people on the spectrum we frequently struggle to see things from other people's perspectives or understand their point of view, so encouraging you to just see things from their point of view can be rather meaningless. However, if you can get someone you trust to work with you to take your current situation and present it to you as a scenario of another company, you may find that it makes more sense. For example, working with someone you trust, they could ask you the question, 'What would you advise a client who came to you with this problem…?' You need to completely turn off in your mind that this relates to you, and take in what they tell you as new information. You are likely to see that your mind processes this information in a different way, and you will be able to provide a very appropriate answer. Take the answer you provided to your friend, and see how you can apply that to your own situation.

Chapter 15

Networking

An On-going Requirement

Frequently, those of us on the autism spectrum take the opportunity to enter business independently as an entrepreneur because we feel this will give us the space we need from other people to cope better and make a better contribution to the business environment by minimising our challenges and optimising the ways we work best. In many respects this is exactly what entrepreneurship does allow us to experience. However, as you have also seen so far, there is still going to be a significant amount of human interaction required of you as you develop you career in this area, irrespective of the format or nature of your business. As Asperger entrepreneurs we need to be able to deal with these situations in ways that do not allow sensory overload issues or other stressors to interfere with our businesses. In this chapter we are going to talk about one activity that can be particularly uncomfortable for us, and this is the activity known as networking.

I believe that the bane of many Asperger entrepreneurs is networking and indirect business development. Most people – neurotypical and Aspergerian – will identify with the fact that we do need to invest time in building new business, but the thought of spending time almost 'socialising' with potential clients is – for the majority of entrepreneurs on the spectrum – something that is considered stressful and superfluous. After all, we have come up with the business idea, we have created the company and initiated contracts or products – why now do we need to waste time chatting with people with no specific business deal or contract as the focus of discussion? Because that is what networking or indirect business development *is*. It is where we invest time connecting with people on a more social level and let them get to know us a little more. Ideally we should also be taking the time to get to know them too, although this tends to be where we experience more challenges than a neurotypical entrepreneur.

When initially asked about their experiences of networking, entrepreneurs on the spectrum being interviewed tended to indicate that this was considered a particularly challenging area. Alison Bruning shared her experience, which is indicative of many people of the spectrum. She says: 'My networking skills come in waves. I had days when I do a lot of networking while other days I couldn't care less. The inconsistency doesn't help my business... My greatest challenge is my inconsistency in doing so. I have a hard time keeping up with all the social media sites. Social interactions are hard for me even though some of my fans, family and friends on Facebook would think otherwise. I can become so fixated on one social site that I neglect my other ones.'

Simon, also an entrepreneur, shared another frustration experienced by the entrepreneurial networker, 'I hate business networking!' he said. 'It's my biggest handicap and I (hate to admit it) resent people who aren't as good as me but manage to work their way up the ladder both in career and money terms.'

Stewart Rapley stated:

Networking just didn't work for me. At meetings I rarely got into any meaningful conversations. When I did I then found that I was hopeless at 'selling'. Being on the spectrum definitely blocked this as an effective route. The direct marketing was a complete failure also! However, I suspect this is tough at the best of times, so I don't think it was caused by me being on the spectrum. Networking among people I already know, however, was much more effective. The career management support [I received] was a good investment as it helped me to develop some 'methods' in my networking. A more structured approach which helps me to be clear on what meeting objectives are etc. has been invaluable.

Entrepreneur Alex focused on a slightly different angle in sharing his experience of networking: 'In my first attempts to network the main challenge was (and still is) the fear of rejection. Of course, while this sometimes happens, the amount of people that will reciprocate is surprising. However, the key is to first ask yourself, "How can they benefit from me within their network?" As is true in life anywhere else, one must be willing to offer something to those you feel would be valuable in your network. Some other challenges for me are how to engage in "casual speak" and expecting others to be "available" freely.'

Gwyneth shares, 'I am very disappointed with it. As a recluse, I don't really know anyone outside very narrow spheres of interest. My personal network has historically been mostly online; not helpful as most of the people I know in the field don't even live in the same country as me.'

Gwyneth's comment raises the topic of networking online through social media, and this is something we will cover later in the chapter. But I will first examine the process of networking in more detail. For the majority of you reading this book, networking is an activity the definition of which you are likely to be familiar with. But for anyone who is less familiar, let me now define networking and explain its importance within a business.

What is networking?

A formal definition of networking obtained from the Oxford dictionary reads: 'Networking is a group of people who exchange information and contacts for professional or social purposes'. (Oxford English Dictionary 2010). However, I prefer the definition which can be found in the small business dictionary on the www.entrepreneur.com website. In defining networking, this reads: 'Developing and using contacts made in business for the purposes beyond the reason for the initial contact'.

The latter definition I believe to offer a far clearer description of what we are actually seeking to do as part of a networking experience. Networking involves building business relationships so that you are able to share information and get them to share information with you.

Examples of networking are where people meet at a conference, and end up sharing details because the one person has shared that they know a potential client who is looking for a consultant to complete a piece of work that the other networker would be able to do. Another example is where two people attend a formal networking event where they end up sharing details because they discover that they have very similar backgrounds and could potentially work together on some of the new projects coming onto the market.

Networking in the last decade has also expanded to include online networking through social media. The definition of online networking is basically the undertaking of networking through the internet for the purposes of increasing your visibility and status, as well as to promote your brand.

The importance of networking for entrepreneurs

Irrespective of how successful your business has become or is in the process of becoming, it is always essential to continue to ensure future business. Unlike larger organisations, smaller or individual businesses generally do not have the time, resources or budget to undertake extensive advertising or general marketing. We need to find other ways to ensure that our business is visible and accessible to the marketplace.

Of course, this does not mean that individual businesses will not undertake other marketing activities, as you will have seen in previous chapters. However, for entrepreneurs it is even more important than for larger businesses that business development is not restricted to these activities.

If you think about a potential client – be they an individual or a company – looking to develop a business relationship with a new supplier that is a large organisation, you would expect them to look at things such as what the potential supplier can offer them financially, the company's credit history, and any recommendations or complaints from other clients. When potential clients are dealing with an entrepreneur, on the other hand, they tend to want to see that individual's brand – something we have already discussed earlier in the book – and understand far more about that person themselves. People recognise that the success of smaller businesses is strongly correlated to the strengths, vision and abilities of the entrepreneur running them, and they will want to be able to have some sort of access to that person's profile.

Some entrepreneurs feel that this requirement can be addressed by making their brand more visible online or through their stationery, offices or other public-facing areas. Certainly this will make a difference, but when it comes down to it, individuals dealing with entrepreneurs prefer much more personal input. Frequently, a person looking for a supplier will be significantly influenced by the impression that an entrepreneur makes face-to-face in a networking event. After all, it is showing that potential client that the entrepreneur can handle him- or herself professionally, is presentable, and is knowledgeable in a way that the potential client feels comfortable with.

That is not to say that they will always need to have met with the entrepreneur themselves, but they place a high value on recommendations where the referee has actually met with the entrepreneur.

Another aspect of networking that is so important for entrepreneurs is that working relationships are strongly influenced by how well the potential client and the potential supplier match each other. Does the potential supplier fit the culture of the client company? If they undertake some work for them as a service provider, do they have compatible visions in so far as ethics, operations and objectives? If they are to supply some products, do their policies and procedures meet the expectations of the clients in areas such as risk, health and safety and green practices?

Networking provides an opportunity for potential clients to speak to the entrepreneur and get a feel for the culture in the entrepreneur's company, and the philosophy and vision of the entrepreneur him- or herself. This will go a long way towards reassuring the client that the entrepreneur is the type of supplier who they could work with successfully. This is the not the kind of reassurance that a client can get from an impersonal online presence, or any type of marketing. Even if there is an indication of this in the marketing or branding, the levels of affirmation of this will never be as high as that provided through networking.

However, perhaps one of the most important elements of networking is that of visibility. By attending things such as conferences and seminars as an entrepreneur, you will have the opportunity to build a presence within the marketplace in your area of specialisation. People will start to associate you with the industry, and when speaking opportunities or supplier contracts arise, they will also begin to think of you. In this way, you will be raising the profile of your business.

Optimal networking in practice

So now we know how networking is defined and why it is important for us to make it part of our business activities, we need to think about the best ways in which to undertake it.

As mentioned previously, networking is not purely about attending events and being visible, it is about the impression you make on people you interact with when you are there, and the ultimate potential for additional information to be obtained as a result of that interaction. In fact, this is the main reason why many of us with Asperger's groan inwardly at the thought of networking – it depends so much on the impression you make on others. Networking is an activity that is built on communication, both verbal and non-verbal, and as such it is one of those areas we possibly need to work at more than neurotypical entrepreneurs.

So why is it that Asperger entrepreneurs find this activity so challenging? The most obvious answer to this is that it is an activity that is people-focused. It relies on the ability to build relationships and hold informal conversations – both of which are things that do not necessarily come naturally to us. It is something that we need to work on, and as such these are activities during which we frequently find ourselves becoming overloaded. As a person on the spectrum who has held a senior position within the corporate world, you will have already developed (in all likelihood) the levels of corporate people skills required for the internal business environment. But, as we have already seen, these requirements are subtly different within a small company. In addition, these 'large company' people skills are not the same as those needed in networking, although some elements do overlap.

There is one way in which communication and people liaison within a small company varies significantly to that of a large company. The following case study highlights this difference.

Case study: Geoffrey's networking experiences

Geoffrey W. is an entrepreneur who started his own financial advisory business after having worked as a financial advisor within one of the financial services businesses in London. It had always been a requirement of his corporate job that he attend conferences and seminars on relevant topics, and networking tended to be a required activity during these events. As a consequence, Geoffrey had learned to deal with networking requirements by mimicking his senior banking peers. Following their approach, he would allow people to approach him, introduce themselves and start a conversation. He then had a relatively standard string of questions that he would ask the other person, which he would ask and then allow the other person to answer. At the end of this, he would present another question, and so on, allowing the person he was networking with to effectively do all the talking. This had worked well for him and, despite the fact that networking was something he really felt he became stressed undertaking, he was able to manage successfully.

Finally making the decision to start his own advisory business, Geoffrey was excited to be free of his corporate constraints. He felt incredibly liberated, and wanted to make certain that his new business was as successful as his business unit in his corporate career had been. He therefore determined to attend some of the key events he knew his peers would be attending during the year so that he could network with them to let them know he was in business for himself.

Confident in his networking strategies, Geoffrey began to mingle after the morning session. Initially, Geoffrey was a bit surprised that no-one came forward to speak with him in the way he was used to. He stood towards the centre of the reception area, but most of the people seemed to be moving to and liaising with some of his old colleagues and associates from the banks and financial services organisations. Geoffrey wasn't used to being – what he considered – ignored. He began to feel self-conscious and irritated, and so made a move to approach a small group of people already speaking.

'Hello, I'm Geoffrey W…' he interrupted, 'I used to work at [name of company] but I'm not there any more.'

The group he had approached seemed surprised by the way he joined them, but they nodded at him politely before continuing their conversation. Geoffrey waited for a break in the conversation before taking the opportunity to look at one of the group and pose a question.

'So why did you come to this conference today?' he asked. The man hesitated a moment, glancing at the others in the networking group, and then proceeded to answer the question briefly. Geoffrey stared at him as he spoke, considering the next question he could raise. The man stopped speaking and Geoffrey took his chance. 'Do you come to the conference every year?'

Geoffrey was so intent on following his established pattern of networking that he did not notice that the rest of the networking group were beginning to wander away, and that the man he was speaking to was beginning to frown and glance around him. He had just started to ask another question when the man interrupted him. 'I'm sorry, I've just seen someone I know.' With that the man moved past him and made his way to the other side of the room. As he watched, Geoffrey saw the man make his way to the bar and order himself a drink, keeping his back to the conference hall. He obviously hadn't moved away to meet anyone. Geoffrey was dumb-founded, having never experienced someone walking out on his conversation before. He felt overwhelmed by the experience, worrying what he had done wrong and wondering what he should do next. It felt like people were giving him a wide berth, and he felt vulnerable and exposed.

Eventually another person came over to speak with him. Geoffrey sighed inwardly – perhaps the previous person was an unusual exception to the rule. 'Hi,' the second networker said, 'I'm Ian Ducaine, from [national bank]. You're Geoffrey W., from [name of company], right?'

Geoffrey shook his hand, 'That's right, although I'm no longer with [name of company].'

'Oh yes? Where have you moved to?'

'I am with [name of his small business].'

'Oh? I don't know them.'

'No, you wouldn't have heard of them yet. So, why did you attend the conference this year?'

Ian hesitated before responding to Geoffrey's question, and then seemed to lose interest in talking with him. Soon Ian also made his excuses and moved away. Geoffrey took his glass back to the bar and ordered a refill. This was not going the way he expected and his confidence had taken an extreme hit. Slowly he stood and finished his drink, keeping his back to the networking group, until it appeared an appropriate time to leave.

The above case study reflects a situation that many people on the spectrum moving from the corporate world to their own businesses experience. In making the move, people often feel that the skills they have learnt over the years in their large company employment can be readily applied within their small business, but this frequently is not the case at all.

In the above study, Geoffrey was confused by the reactions he received from people he was networking with. His approach had always been acceptable when he was a director within the well-known company who had employed him previously, so why wasn't it appropriate for him afterwards?

One of the main things to observe in Geoffrey's approach to networking is that he was acting as if he was still a high profile director in a well-known organisation. What do I mean by this? Well, when you are a director in a high profile and sought after international company, suppliers would do anything to get in front of you. You are the doorway into a very valuable organisation, and as a consequence people will tend to be very eager to please you, or say and do what you expect. You are the one who is expecting to grant a favour in the networking relationship, and as such you do not have that much work to do. The name and reputation of your employer does most of that for you.

When you become an entrepreneur, on the other hand, you are the one who is seeking to find the 'doorway' into potential clients. You no longer have the invisible backing of a large company name behind you. The impression you make on people from this point onward will be 100 per cent you. Therefore, the way you speak to people needs to change. If you look at Geoffrey's approach, you will see that the way he tried to speak with people as he networked was characterised by the 'what can you do for me?' inflection as opposed to one of 'what can I do for you?' This is a subtle but extremely important difference. No longer are you waiting for and expecting the other person to lead the conversation and do most of the talking. Now that pleasure falls to you. You need to drive and direct the conversation in such a way that is not seen as pushy by the other party, and in a way that is engaging and positive – reflecting you and your new company in a positive light.

You need to be able to inspire confidence in the potential client in front of you far more than you would have ever needed to do as a corporate employee. For many people – both neurotypical and autistic – this can result in stress as individuals try to work out how they need to change their approach. It isn't always that obvious – especially for those of us on the spectrum.

So let's go back to basics and think about what is involved in being a successful networker within a small business environment. After that, we can discuss what that requirement may involve for those of us on the spectrum, and then consider some tactics to ensure that we are successful in this key activity.

Defining networking as a core entrepreneurial activity

Networking as an activity is essential for small business owners, no matter what form that networking takes. There are several reasons that this is so important for the small business, but the most obvious one is that it tends to be a significant source of potential new business leads. However, it is also important for you as a business owner, since it provides you with the opportunity to develop different sorts of working relationships.

There are really five types of network that are valuable for you as an entrepreneur. These are:

- business development networks
- operational networks
- strategic networks
- personal support networks
- social media networks.

The last of these types can but doesn't always encompass all of the other four types. If we think about these network types, what they are is quite clear to see from their description, but let me be explicit. The *business development networks* are those that individuals develop specifically to seek out and win new business. The types of event that encourage business development networks forming are supplier-led workshops, fairs and demonstration events.

Operational networks, on the other hand, are networks which serve to provide you with valuable contacts who can provide assistance and insights into some of your operational issues. For example, you may set up contact with some people who are IT specialists or finance specialists, and you could share useful information between yourselves. Your IT contact could help you with some advice about setting up your network, while you could advise them on the legal situation of their new venture (depending on your area of expertise, of course).

Strategic networks are those that provide you with valuable contacts in respect of the growth of your company, such as people worth contacting in the venture capital world. *Personal support networks* are also very important, although it is recognised that this may be an area where many people on the spectrum fall short. Having a network of people you know and trust on a personal level is very important. These are the people we can turn to when we have a bad day (or week!) to let off steam and have a rant, without fear of being judged or having our credibility as a business person questioned. These are generally the people who know about the fact we are on the spectrum and encourage us and are there for us. For those people who are fortunate enough to have such a network *as well as* to use it, a personal network can be invaluable.

The final type of network is the *social media network*. For those of us on the spectrum, this can actually turn out to be the most valuable network of them all, and many ASD entrepreneurs already make considerable use of it. The social media network includes such areas as Bebo, Facebook, MySpace, YouTube and so on. More business-specific online networking sites include LinkedIn, Xing, and Twitter. Additional methods of networking online include developing a business blog of your own, or by creating eBooks or webinars. These are extremely useful for those of us who experience a challenge in undertaking face-to-face networking, since it can allow you to develop an excellent profile in the marketplace ahead of any actual physical networking. Webinars or video on a YouTube business page can be an excellent way for people to get to see you visually, without you necessarily having to be overwhelmed by the sights of several other people all focusing on you.

However, irrespective of how useful online networking is, it should only be considered as a stepping stone to your direct face-to-face networking, since this is where you will make your greatest impact and potentially win business.

I have been invited to a business event where I know I will need to network – so now what?

OK, so we now have an idea of what networking is and why it is so important to us as entrepreneurs. Many autistic people feel that this really does not help them, since they feel overwhelmed by the requirements of networking and feel it is too big to handle. I believe that if the process of networking is simplified into some manageable steps, this will make it much easier for you to cope with and undertake, despite not being a neurotypical. What follows are some networking strategies that you can use to make the event less stressful and enable you to feel more in control. Let's start by breaking the networking event down into some manageable chunks.

There are three main parts to networking, together with an additional step that is specific to people on the spectrum, and each of these will have a number of steps. I will walk you through those steps as we progress and by the end of the chapter, you will have more confidence that you will be able to handle your next networking event. I have tried to make the format of the chapter more procedural, so that you can try to start thinking of networking as a process rather than a stressful encounter with others. I know that for myself, turning the networking into a visual flow-chart in my mind helps me get through.

What follows is a one page flow-chart that I use as a mind-map to focus on during any networking encounter. I encourage you to develop something similar for yourself, or to use the one provided here if you find it helpful. I have included a copy of this in Toolkit Exercise 8, and you will also be able to download a copy of this from www.jkp.com/catalogue/book/9781849055093/resources.

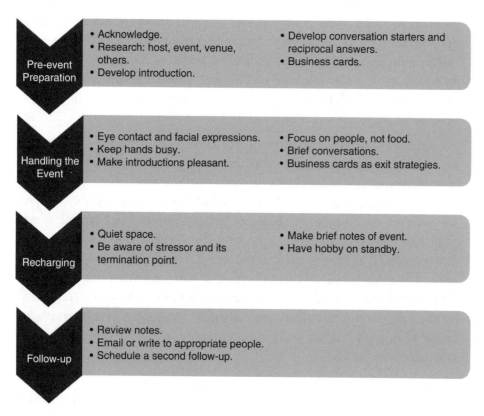

Figure 15.1: The Networking Flow-Chart

From this flow chart you will see that there are four stages to the networking process: *Pre-event preparation, Handling the event, Recharging time* and *Follow-up.*

Pre-event preparation

1. *Acknowledge the invitation* – The first step in networking is actually getting somewhere that gives you the opportunity to undertake these activities. So receiving an invitation to attend some type of networking event is an important first step in the process. Many people who are uncomfortable or unfamiliar with networking lose out by failing to actually attend events where they would have the chance to network. I can almost guarantee you that if you are uncomfortable with networking, the receipt of an invitation to an event will fill you with utter dread! However, don't spend time thinking about this. Instead, try to check your schedule for your availability at that time as soon as you can, and if you are available – book it! Commit yourself to the event by sending through an RSVP or an email confirming that you will be attending. You may be incredibly tempted to cancel, but try to ensure that you honour your commitment to attend, possibly by reminding yourself that not attending would be the same as letting the person who invited you down.

2. *Research the person or organisation that invited you* – Do an internet search of the person or the organisation that sent you an invitation. This can provide you with some valuable insights into the sorts of things that may be worth finding out more about ahead of the meeting, or about topics of conversation that may perhaps not be appropriate. For example, if you find that the company that is hosting the event is one that has taken a public stand against genetic engineering, you certainly would need to ensure that this is a subject area that you do not get involved in discussing. This sort of research may also give you an idea as to why you were invited to the event in the first place, such as the host company planning to start some work in the region and looking to develop relationships with small companies in the area.

3. *Research the event and venue* – If this is a particular event that you have been invited to as opposed to a more general networking event, try to find out some more about the event, as well as the venue it is being held at. If it is a particular event, there may be certain areas of knowledge or current affairs that you would be expected to be familiar with. Entrepreneur Simon highlights why this is so important when he says: 'If I'm confident about an area of expertise, I am confident to present it to clients. I believe it's my obsessions that help with this. If I need to know about something, I tend to get anxious and worked up about it until I am comfortable with my knowledge of the subject.' If you have done your research beforehand,

there is far less potential for you to become overwhelmed at an event due to being concerned that you do not have sufficient knowledge to engage properly. I can identify completely with Simon's comment, since I too can be totally stressed if I feel people are talking about something I do not know as much about as I feel is appropriate for me. We do tend to set high standards for ourselves, though. Remember that people in a networking environment are generally not expecting you to be an expert in everything – even if that's what we consider necessary for ourselves!

It is also important to research the venue, because it may give you some clues about dress code (if this is not explicit in the invitation). For example, being invited to a networking event that turns out to be at a polo match is very different to being invited to a black tie event in the evening. Spend a few minutes finding out about the venue and the types of event generally held there and you will feel more confident on the day. If there is some ambiguity in this area, do not be concerned about going back to your host (or whoever invited you) and asking them the dress code for the day. It is not an unusual query and can often be seen as very proactive on your side.

4. *Research others attending* – If you have access to the details of other people attending the same event, try to get some publicly available information on them. Look them up on the social media sites, or do a search for them on the internet. This will help you not only in being aware of who is attending, but also to be a little bit knowledgeable about things of interest to them that you could discuss if you happen to meet during the networking. That said, it is important to be aware of the sorts of things to raise in a conversation and those that really should not be raised. Do be aware that it is always inadvisable to talk about politics, personal matters and recent tragic events (such as a death in the family, etc). The sorts of things you could discuss would be things like an interesting hobby, if you find they have worked somewhere you have in the past, if they have written a book or been given an award.

5. *Develop your introduction* – I was once advised by someone (and I do wish I could remember who, so that I could fully acknowledge their insight!) that a trick to making a good impression in a networking session was to prepare a short introduction to yourself to use as part of your greeting. This would usually be one or two sentences. So, for example, my introduction could be, 'Hello, I'm Rosalind Bergemann, Chairman of Asperger Leaders. I mentor business leaders who are on the autism spectrum.' As this friend told me, the whole point of this is that the person you are addressing

would then have their interest sparked enough to want to know more about you and your business. I think that this is a wonderful idea, but I would perhaps add to this in a couple of ways: first, I would say that you not only need to develop your introduction, you also need to have thought about some answers to any questions this may evoke. Second, I would suggest you actually think about two or perhaps three versions of your introduction, since it frequently happens at networking events that an additional person will come and join your conversation part way through, and you will stop to introduce yourself to them. It isn't really appropriate to use the same introduction that you have used to someone else standing right there, because they will then become aware that you are reading from a script and may lose interest in speaking further with you.

If you are then in a situation where perhaps a fourth person joins you, it would then be acceptable to re-use an introduction, starting this by saying something to the effect of, 'As I said to John, my name is…'

6. *Develop some conversation-starter questions and your reciprocal responses* – You will recall from the case study earlier in the chapter that Geoffrey had learned to cope with networking by developing a set of questions for the people he was speaking to. This is not a bad strategy, per se, but it will only be useful if properly used. You will need to make sure that you not only develop some 'opener' question, but that you are able to carry on the reciprocal conversation. For example, a common question could be along the lines of 'So, have you worked here in Boston before?' Let's hope, the person will say yes and you can ask for more information. But they may well say, 'No, what about you?' Now the conversation has reversed and it is up to you to provide the answers and keep the listener interested. It isn't necessary to have a library of potential questions and answers. You will probably do fine with five or six standard questions that you know will need some sort of detailed response (as opposed to the 'yes' or 'no' type). What is also important for you to remember is to alternate your opener questions with different people. You never know who is standing behind you in a networking environment. Repeating the same questions in the same order to another person that you have just presented to someone who is standing nearby may very well make them feel that your networking is artificial or forced, and they may lose interest in future networking or business opportunities with you.

7. *Ensure you have adequate supplies of business cards and other necessities* – It may sound like an obvious thing to say, but ensuring that you have adequate supplies to things like business cards is really important. There is

nothing worse than realising the morning of the event that you don't have business cards and that they can only be printed in three days' time! Also, on the day of the event, make sure that you have enough of things such as handkerchiefs or tissues, a spare set of contact lenses, touch-up make-up and so forth.

Handling the event

1. *Eye contact and facial expressions* – I don't need to tell you that this is an area where a large percentage of us tend to have some challenges. The main things that you need to keep in mind are that you should try to keep a smile on your face when you introduce yourself, and that you should try to keep regular eye contact. Beware, though, of ending up staring at people. Regular eye contact means that you occasionally look away (for example, at your glass or anything in your hand), but return your eyes to theirs when they speak. It is always a good idea, if this is an area you are challenged with, to practise in front of a mirror or ask someone that you trust to have a practice networking session with you so that they can give you some feedback. The most important requirements are that you smile, introduce yourself and offer your hand for a handshake. Firm, brief handshakes are best – avoid limp, cripplingly tight or 'shoulder breaking' handshakes. Just one or two firm shakes and then let go.

2. *Keep your hands busy* – Another important suggestion that may be particularly important for those of us on the spectrum (although by no means restricted to us) is that you keep something in your hands. When I say to keep something in your hands, I do not mean something large or unwieldy. It needs to be something relatively inconspicuous and comfortable for you to hold while in conversation with someone else. Examples here would be a tea cup, a wine glass, a plate with a couple of nibbles on it (see my note later on about eating while networking), or a brochure. It needs to be something that you are able to hold comfortably while shaking hands with a person you are being introduced to, so things like large books, multiple paper or large plates of food would be inappropriate.

   The reason that I recommend you hold something in your hands (or hand, as the case may be) is that most people don't really know what to do with their hands if they are just standing around. People can end up folding their arms (a very defensive gesture), putting their hands in their pockets (seen as a scruffy or careless look) or even just clasping their hands together in front of them (often seen as an unconfident look). In addition, some of us on the spectrum have a tendency to stim when we are nervous, which means that we may make repetitive movements with our arms or hands, such as drumming our fingers on our legs, swinging our arms slightly or even what they call 'flapping'. Most of the time we don't even realise we are doing this. Sometimes this can be highly distracting for other people, and will put people off coming to speak with us. Holding something comfortably in your hand will make you look more comfortable and hence more approachable.

3. *Make introductions pleasant* – Again, if you have a look at Geoffrey's experience in the case study once more, you will see that this is not always as straightforward as it seems. Some essentials for you to keep in mind when making introductions are:

   a. When joining a group, never interrupt someone speaking or just join the conversation. Always wait for an appropriate moment and then introduce yourself before adding any comments. The only exception to this general rule is when you are finding it challenging to find a 'point of entrance' into the conversation. Sometimes you need to join by acknowledging the comment of another person before introducing yourself. For example, making the comment, 'I couldn't agree more with you. My name is Rosalind Bergemann, by the way. I'm a management consultant in the area of change.' In this way you have gently interrupted the discussion to get into the conversation.

   b. Make sure that you give your attention to all participants in the conversation at appropriate times, not just one.

4. *Focus on people, not food* – Here is another consideration which frequently isn't considered by networkers. If you are attending an event where there are light refreshments during networking, make sure that you are not focusing more on the food than you are on the networking. Again, this is not a comment that I would make exclusively to people on the spectrum. Neurotypicals can be just as naive about this as anyone. Think about it. People trying to have a conversation with someone really do not enjoy watching them eat while they speak to them. Also, beware of over-eating. You are there to network, not for a meal.

   It is always a good idea to have something to eat before you attend a networking event, even if there are refreshments as part of it. This ensures that you are not distracted by the sight or smell of the food. I recommend that if you are attending an event that has a buffet or refreshments of sorts, that you take one or two small items onto your plate, together with a napkin. Use your plate as your item to keep in your hand, and rather focus on speaking to people than specifically eating anything. You could discretely 'nibble' at your food, possibly when other people in the networking group are speaking to each other, rather than to you. Above all else, make sure that you avoid shaking hands after having handled food without wiping your hand on your napkin first.

5. *Hold brief conversations* – Networking works by allowing people the opportunity to meet new people and exchange details. What you don't need to do is to turn the event into a minor meeting by making your conversations too long. As a guideline, you should be speaking to individuals (or a small group of people) for no more than 15 minutes. After that time you need to move on to someone else by utilising your exit strategy, as described below.

6. *Exchange business cards as an exit strategy* – Once you have completed your conversation, it is important that you exit from the conversation in an efficient and amiable manner. The best way to do this is to initiate the exchange of business cards, because most people recognise this as a signal that the meeting has come to a close. Find an appropriate time in the conversation to break eye contact, look into your purse or look to your pocket to retrieve a business card, and say something like, 'Let me give you one of my business cards…' At this point the person or people you are speaking to will generally reciprocate by offering you theirs. End the conversation by saying that it was nice speaking with them.

Recharging time

For those of us on the spectrum, a networking event is without doubt going to be a challenging occurrence. In order for us to regain our composure and effectively recover from the networking event, it is generally a good idea for you to build into your schedule some time to recharge. Never make the mistake of scheduling another meeting or important activity after your networking event. In reality, you are highly unlikely to be up to facing it and if you do, you are likely to experience quite a bit of additional stress.

What follows are some suggestions on how to prepare for a recharging session in the best way.

1. *Have a quiet space prepared or made ready for you* – If you are attending a networking session, try to ensure beforehand that you have an 'escape area' prepared for afterwards. If you are not going straight home after the event,

this can be an office or meeting room at your workplace that you should ensure you formally book. If you are going home straight afterwards and have a family, make certain that they are aware that you need some alone time and are not to be disturbed for an agreed period of time.

2. *Be aware of the stressor, but know it is controllable* – Be aware that networking events can be stressors for you, and accept that this is not a fault on your side: it is just part of who you are. It doesn't help to try to imagine that you are not going to be affected by this, or condone yourself for your perceived failures in the networking arena. Instead, know it *will* be challenging, but be confident that you have coping strategies in place and that you are the type of person who can overcome a challenge successfully. At the end of the event, be reassured that the stressor is over and therefore you are able to move on from this. Congratulate yourself on a job well done. We know it isn't easy, but you faced it and made it through. Using the strategies in this chapter, let's hope it will not be as stressful as it might have previously been.

3. *Consider making brief notes* – When you are in your quiet place, you may want to think about taking some time to make brief notes about the people you have met and want to follow up with. You will be surprised at how quickly a person can forget important information when it has been obtained in a difficult or uncomfortable environment. I have found it useful to have a pre-prepared paper which I can then just populate, or complete as I start to relax. I have included a template of this in Toolkit Exercise 9.

4. *Have a hobby on standby* – There is absolutely no better way to unwind and clear your mind of any residual negative effects of a stressor than to make use of a special hobby, especially for most of us on the spectrum. Things like reading, building things, computer games, pets or studying – whatever your special interest is – they are all valuable to us because we enjoy doing them and we relax as we do them. I have sometimes used the thought of one of my hobbies as a motivator to get me through a particularly intense networking session, and I have found this a very strong form of encouragement for me. Think about how you can use your own hobbies and areas of special interest to work for you in this area.

Follow-up

1. *Review your notes* – Once you have had the opportunity to recharge your resources and feel back to where you should be, you should find time to

review your notes for the event. Now that you are thinking more clearly (in the autistic overload sense!), you can think about any additional points you want to add to your original notes, such as impressions that you were given by certain people, or important observations you made about the way the person communicated with you. Let me give you an example here of what I am talking about, because it is important to be clear about what we mean.

Case study: Karen's networking impression list

Karen attended her first networking event last month, and had struggled to get through it. Despite her initial fears, however, she did manage to get through, although she took quite a while to recover. While she was going through her recharging phase, she made some initial notes about the people she had spoken with and their companies. She thought she had been quite thorough in doing so and that she had enough details to inform her decisions regarding follow-up.

A week after her event, Karen met up with someone she had been a friend with while working. She shared with her friend about the challenges she experienced in the networking event, but also happily shared that she had been able to gather the information she needed to decide about further contact.

'That's great, Karen,' her friend Alison shared, 'so which of them are you going to contact?'

Karen pulled out her notes and started to scan through them. There were seven or eight of them with very similar profiles, and she shared with her friend that she felt that she would contact these people.

'Wow,' Alison laughed, 'That's quite a few people. Which ones made you feel the most at ease – maybe you can approach them first?'

Karen frowned. At ease? That wasn't something she had thought about.

'Well,' she said slowly, 'I suppose this one made me feel a bit uncomfortable because he kept speaking over me, and this one actually made me feel really out of place by mentioning that I hadn't worn a cocktail dress...'

'Well, why on earth would you want to contact them?' Alison shook her head in surprise. Karen paused.

'Actually, I don't think I do. I would much rather make contact with *this* person, because she and I seemed to get on really well, and I wouldn't mind speaking with her again...'

The previous example reflects some of the additional areas you should try to recall once you have relaxed enough to recollect the event in more detail. I know that considering feelings or emotions is not necessarily the easiest thing to do, but these are not the only considerations. Others are whether the person was abrupt or short with you, whether they appeared excessively loud, whether they were possibly drinking a lot at the event that made you uncomfortable and so forth. After all, these are people with whom you could potentially be working in the future. Keep this in mind as you think of them.

2. *Email or write to people who shared their business cards* – Once you have decided who you want to make contact with, send them a note within the first few days of the event to make contact and thank them for the time they spent speaking with you. If you have a street address for the person, try to send this as a hard-copy letter, since this tends to make more of an impression and is more likely to be read than an email. However, if you do only have an email address, do still send your email.

   Your initial communication should be brief, just thanking them for their time and sharing that it was good to meet them. Tell them you enjoyed speaking with them and that perhaps you will make contact in the future to speak some more. Invite them to contact you if they have anything they would like to discuss.

3. *Schedule a second follow up with key people* – About four to six week later, it is appropriate to then contact these people again as a second follow up if you haven't been touch already. Be prepared this time to invite them to join you for a coffee or for lunch. Two important points to note here are the following:

   a. First, you are inviting them for coffee or lunch. Do not become a nag. If they do not respond, it is time to leave it for a while.

   b. If you make an appointment to meet, *keep it!* It can sometimes be very tempting to cancel at the last moment because the thought of more networking is so worrying. However, you need to see this through.

Some basic elements of body language to consider

Finally, I would like to briefly cover a very important consideration when it comes to networking, that of body language. Reading body language for those of us who have an autism spectrum disorder can sometimes be extremely challenging. It can be an area of weakness for us, and although we may have sufficiently mastered this to operate well within the corporate world, the stresses of attending a networking event can sometimes make our self-conditioning go out the window, as they say.

I am going to list a few body language 'markers' that it is important for you to be aware of in the networking environment.

Negative body language

When you are speaking with someone, you need to be aware of when they start to display negative body language, because this could very well be their way of trying to tell you that they are tired of the conversation or do not want to continue to network with you right then. If you ignore the body signals people are giving you, people can become irritated, annoyed or even downright angry with you, believing that you are ignoring the signals on purpose.

So what are some of the most common negative body cues that you should try to keep alert for?

LOSS OF EYE CONTACT

Loss of eye contact from a neurotypical always indicates a negative signal if they had been having reasonable eye contact with you before. As people on the spectrum, we are sometimes less aware of this being an issue because we have to force ourselves to remember to make eye contact. Therefore, someone not making eye contact actually feels more genuine to us! However, do keep in mind that failure to make good eye contact is not the exclusive realm of people on the spectrum. Sometimes neurotypicals who are introverted or shy can be just as eye-elusive. What you need to look out for is a *change* from eye contact to lack of eye contact. This is the negative signal.

FOLDING ARMS

When people suddenly fold their arms across their chests and stop talking as much as they were, this is a sign that the person is not comfortable talking to you – for whatever reason. Again, you need to be aware that this does not mean every occurrence of folding arms is a negative one. You need to take the context into account. Say for example that you are standing outside networking. The woman you are talking to is wearing a light blouse and no jacket. As you talk, the weather takes a turn for the worse and the wind picks up. If the woman folds her arms across her chest at this time, it is in all likelihood because she is cold, not because she is not comfortable speaking with you.

Any of the following additional signs are what you should look for if you see the person fold their arms over their chest:

- Have they stopped conversing as much as they were?

- Are they leaning away from you, or turning their body away from you?

- Are they frowning?

- Are they sighing or losing eye contact?

If you notice any of these, take it that this is a negative body signal and move on.

TURNING AWAY OF THE BODY

Another negative body signal is when people start to turn their bodies away from you so that they are not facing you properly. This can sometimes be easy to miss if you are concentrating on having a good conversation.

The best way to check is to glance at the person's shoulders. Are they facing towards you or in your direction, or is one shoulder behind the other – almost as if the person is beginning to turn away from you in slow motion? This can either be the person indicating to you that they want to move on or that they want to speak with someone else. Again, take context into account. If the person is likely to be turning because the sun is in their eyes, this is not the same situation.

INTRUSION OF PERSONAL SPACE

Although this may not sound like a negative, one thing that can sometimes go wrong at a networking event is that a person could try to become personal when you are trying to be professional. We need to be aware that sometimes we may not pick up when someone starts flirting with us. The best way to avoid this is to keep the concept of personal space in mind.

Most of us on the spectrum are not comfortable with people being too close to us – it just comes with the territory. As a businessperson and someone with a family, many of us have had to learn to overcome our aversion and to just cope with the feelings. Because of this, we may actually have made ourselves insensitive to people stepping into our personal space inappropriately, and rather than reacting as a neurotypical would, we automatically tell ourselves that we are being oversensitive and that we need to just put up with the negative feelings.

I recommend that you try to keep the following in mind to help you determine if you have someone possibly trying to get overly personal with you:

- The definition of personal space will vary depending on where in the world you live. In most western cultures, personal space is seen as the space surrounding you up to an arm's length or about half a metre. People coming within this are violating your personal place.

- Be aware of your environment. Could the person be moving closer to you because it is very noisy and they are trying to hear you? If so, do you need to speak louder so that they can move back?

- Does the person possibly have a hearing difficulty? Have you noticed if they move closer to everyone they speak to?

- Does the person appear to be smiling a lot, and looking up at you from a lowered head (if she is a woman) or down at you with eyes that are not wide open (if you are a woman)?

- If you move away from them, do they move forward again?

- Are their eyes making contact with your body at times rather than your eyes?

If you are at a networking event and you are not interested in any personal relationships developing as a result (which I am sure you are not!), then now is the time to make a professional exit and move on. Do *not* offer them your business card, but rather say that you need to mingle some more, and that it was good speaking to them. Don't wait for a response, but move on immediately.

While the chapter has ended by discussing some of the smaller challenges of networking, do keep in mind that this is an important area of your business development as well as of your personal growth. As you continue to network, some of the strategies and factors I have highlighted for you to be aware of will become second nature to you, and the process will – believe it or not – become easier. You may never become completely comfortable with the process of networking – many of us never do – but the important thing is that none of the people you network with will ever be able to tell that, and the success you have within your business as a result of your contacts will certainly make you feel that it was worth all the effort you have put into it.

Chapter 16

Making your New Business the Focus in your Life

NOT your Life in Totality

Someone once made a comment to me that took me by surprise. She was one of the few people (at that time) who I had shared my diagnosis with, and we had been working together for about eight months.

'Rosalind,' she said, 'Sometimes I envy you having Asperger's.'

I was taken aback by her obvious sincerity, and asked her why she felt that.

'Well,' she said. 'You guys have such focus and dedication. I mean, if you want something or set your mind to achieving something, you just keep going until you get there!'

I suppose I do understand the point that my colleague was making. At the time, I was involved in running three major work programmes within a global organisation and it was acknowledged that running even one of them could be seen as a significant challenge. But I knew that the organisation needed me to help them with this, and therefore I went out of my way to help them, working ridiculous hours (by neurotypical standards) due to the company being global. I was at work more than I was at home. Fortunately for my daughter she had already left home by then, because my house began to suffer. I didn't have time for things like housekeeping, spring-cleaning or the niceties of making a house a home. I didn't have time to meet any previous work associates, for networking, for professional development, for hobbies. I had made the very common mistake of making my work my life.

My experience is not unique. Alison Bruning shares: 'I have found it hard to have a day to myself so I can recover from a week of dealing with people and social interactions. That's hard for me because I need that time. Also, there's not time to have a meltdown. I have them sometimes when I am over stimulated. People don't understand why I do the things I do when I am in that mood. Knowing that only makes things worse for me.'

But everyone knows you need to make sacrifices...

One of the most common responses from people who have started to overcommit themselves to their new businesses is that it is normal to make sacrifices in order to make a success of your business. And quite right – I agree with you totally. If you are going to start a new business you must expect to make some sacrifices. However, there is a difference between making sacrifices and making your new business your life in totality. This is what I want to discuss in this chapter.

As I have said previously, we as people on the spectrum can often totally immerse ourselves in something if we feel that it requires our attention. However, unlike most neurotypicals, most of us do not have that automatic off switch that triggers almost instinctively to warn a person that they have reached the point that they need to stop. As a result, we can end up continuing far beyond what would be considered healthy self-sacrifice and actually end up making ourselves ill. When we do this, not only does our own health suffer, but inevitably the health of our new business suffers as well.

In order to ensure that long-term health of both ourselves and our companies, we need to make sure that the sacrifices we make are reasonable and intelligent ones and that we have a strategy in place to help us to identify when we are starting to go over that fine line of healthy versus unhealthy commitment. The best way I have found to do this is to make use of the time commitment template (Toolkit Exercise 4.2) that you used as part of Chapter 5. Take a few minutes now to review what you entered into your template before you carry on, and perhaps print a fresh copy from the website.

Making time for family and friends

Now that you have your template, I want you to start – before you consider any work or business commitments, to add some time into your scheduler for family and friends. If you have a family at home, you will need to think about daily commitments. If you live on your own, you will need to think about time to talk to or meet up with family and friends. It is very easy to think along the lines of 'oh well, they'll understand if I can't get in touch as often as I used to'. That is true up to a point. If you do not actively commit time to them, this time will end up getting absorbed into your business, and you will suddenly find that a year has gone by without you having spoken to people you used to have regular contact with. Not only is this difficult for them, this is not good for you, since you will be losing some of your regular support network that way. Take a tip. Block the time off now.

Making time for hobbies and interests

An area that many people sacrifice when they start their own businesses is in the area of hobbies and interests. However, as a person on the spectrum, I want to raise a caution with you on this one. Quite frequently, hobbies and special interests serve a particular role for us. Not only is it something we do because we are particularly interested in it, but frequently we do this because it acts as one of our stress management mechanisms – even if we don't realise it.

When we then decide that we are going to sacrifice this hobby in order to spend more time on our new business, we end up inadvertently eliminating a mechanism we have used previously to relax and unwind. As a result, we may end up becoming overloaded and start to suffer from overload issues.

Therefore, I strongly recommend that you find some time in your schedule for at least one of your regular hobbies or interests. You may find that you have to sacrifice the amount of time you can allocate to this interest, but if you can still have access to it, this should help you enormously.

Beware of over-committing

We all know that to those of us on the spectrum, if we want to make a success of something, we will go out of our way to do so. People who work with us will also frequently pick up on our commitment, dedication and determination, and sadly some people do take advantage of this. When you are working with clients – or even with your team – be very aware of the fact that you could easily over-commit yourself in trying to offer the best that you can.

As an example, if you had a client who asked you to take on some consultancy work in addition to what you have contracted to do, at the same time as completing the original work, in all likelihood most of us would go out of our way to say yes. However, even if we are able to undertake the work, it is likely to be at significant cost to ourselves in terms of our time and energies, and this would probably raise the risk of our becoming overloaded. This would result in our needing time to ourselves, which would result in reduced productivity after this project, which would lead to increased pressures…do you get my drift?

Make certain that when you are considering things like projects, you work with your scheduler in hand. Have a look at your time commitments and those parts you have blocked off as essential. Next consider areas that are more flexible, and make a decision only after having ensured that you have the available time. I would recommend you think about using a scheduler that caters to this sort of decision making, such as the Asperger Leaders' Scheduler, available from Asperger Leaders (www.aspergerleaders.org.uk).

Consider additional resources

Finally, if you are in the very enviable position of finding that you have more work than you can cope with, you will need to consider bringing in additional resources. Keep in mind in doing this, however, that you will also need to allocate time to orientate and train any new starters, so build this time into your schedule as well.

Chapter 17

Developing your Work Area to Optimise your Performance

Possibly one of the most common reasons for people starting their own businesses – not just Aspergerians – is that this provides them with control over their working situation – the type of work, hours of work and working environment. For those of us who have sensory sensitivity issues, this can be seen as a particular blessing. Anyone with sensory hypersensitivities who has spent years in the corporate world battling with the tension and distress of overloads caused by such things as open plan offices, fluorescent lighting and equipment with high-frequency audio outputs will know what I mean by this. For many Aspergerians leaving the corporate world to start their own companies, the first thought is, 'My own space to fit my own needs!' Without a doubt, this is a very important advantage for us in having our own businesses. Unlike an employee, if we need to purchase or lease special equipment, stationery or office space to reduce overload issues, there is nothing to stop us other than financial considerations. We do not have to motivate it to management, or risk disclosure implications by having to motivate it under health and safety or disability rights. We are the boss – we can do as we wish.

In starting up their businesses, however, many people do not actually take their needs in respect of their Asperger traits into consideration – or if they do, they do not align these adequately to the on-going needs of the business. Let us consider an example of a successful corporate accountant with Asperger syndrome who made the decision to start his own accountancy firm.

Case study: David H. and his accountancy firm's office

David H. was a forty-one-year-old chartered accountant diagnosed with Asperger syndrome in his mid-thirties. David had been a highly successful internal accountant within a large multi-national financial services company based in London. Following a very successful year within his company, David received a significant performance-related bonus that empowered him to finally take the step he had yearned to take for many years already – to leave the corporate world and start his own accountancy practice.

Delighted to finally be moving away from the 'corporate monster', David made the decision to also move out of the city, allowing him to avoid that monotonous and stressful commute he had had to endure for so many years. In addition, he was also aware that certain parts of Surrey, the county in which he lived, did not have many professional accountancy firms with large corporate experience, most of them catering to small businesses. This represented a gap in the market, and a good business development opportunity. Many of his accounts contacts lived in Surrey as well, and he was certain there would not be a problem recruiting accountants for his office from the local area. Therefore, David decided to register his company in Surrey, and started to look for office space.

Being eager to get his practice established and offering services, David did not spend a lot of time researching the office space. He knew more or less how much space he would require, and was delighted to find an office space provider that was able to offer him an entire floor of a high profile business address – inclusive of furniture – at a very reasonable price, subject to a five year lease. Without hesitation, David committed to the lease.

Moving into the offices, David was pleased to find that there was a corner office that he was able to use for himself, together with two smaller offices that could be used for the office manager and payroll officer. There were three client meeting rooms, with the rest of the office being open plan. David had made sure that the company looking for office space for him knew that it was a basic requirement for him to have a separate office space. This was the most important element of his work environment, since he had a number of hypersensitivities and felt that being able to close the door and create his own space would be all he needed to reduce any overloads.

The time came for him to move into his new business. Seven accountants had been hired, together with some administrative staff, and David was pleased with how the new office appeared to fit together.

'Finally,' he thought, relaxing behind his desk in his large corner office, 'I can do the work I love without battling against an overload issue every day!'

However, within a few days of starting his new business, David found that things weren't going as smoothly as planned. He realised that he was starting to get tense and hypervigilant during the day, and recognised these as the symptoms of a sensory overload, but he had no idea what was the cause or even which senses were involved. David had been careful to ensure that the offices he rented did not have fluorescent lighting (since this had always been an issue for him) but had a sophisticated system of uplighting, together with glass windows to the outside in the open plan area that stretched from ceiling to floor, thereby allowing in as much light as was possible. He also had his office into which he could retreat and close his door if he felt overloaded by too much noise, but this didn't seem to be helping.

One day David was sitting alone in his office when he reached a point of major overload. He knew he had to get out of the office or at least open a window and get some fresh air. If he wasn't able to do this, he knew himself well enough to recognise that this could interfere with his ability to process any more information that day, or even interact with his staff at all. Getting up, he realised for the first time that his office – and his overall office space – did not have any windows that could be opened, and that in order to leave the office, he would need to walk down the length of the open plan office to reach the reception area. He was not going to do well walking down the length of the open plan office – bustling with activity as it was – the way he was currently feeling, so he sat down again, momentarily at a loss at how to handle his situation. He considered trying to stay where he was, but quickly realised that was not an option since his stress levels were continuing to rise. Desperate, David even thought about making a mad dash down the centre of the office just to get out. Fortunately, he remembered that the fire escape was closer than the reception area, so made his way out onto the fire escape landing on the outside of the building.

Hands and body trembling, David stood gripping the handrail and breathing deeply. Standing outside with street noises floating up to him – something he would ordinarily find distracting and irritating –

David found himself slowly starting to de-stress. He also realised that, despite being outside, the area where he was standing on the fire escape actually appeared to be quieter than his office with the door closed. David took some time to think about that, and realised that the enclosed office he had seen as essential for himself could potentially be the cause of his problems. He recalled that there was an air-conditioning unit in there, and realised that without any windows all the humming from the unit was echoing off the walls, and therefore coming at him from all directions in an amplified manner. He also realised that the lighting in his office was not as good as that in the open plan area due to the fact that the uplighter used a type of lamp that created a contrast against the walls without the benefit of any natural light, and this resulted in an unusually intense environment. There was also no facility to dim the brightness of the lamp. And there was no doubting the fact that his office was so far from the practice's reception and exit was an issue, as he had only realised on having to leave the office at a difficult time. Because he knew he had his own office, he had not even thought about having some sort of breakaway area aside from this.

David sighed and rubbed his eyes. He had a five year lease on his office space, and now it appeared that this could be worse than his environment in the corporate world! What had he signed up for?

As the above case study highlights, a lack of insight into how the environment affects you can have significant consequences when you make the decision to operate from your own business offices. Even if you are aware of how your current office environment negatively (or positively!) affects you, that may not necessarily be sufficient to ensure that choice of office going forward is challenge-free, or at the least has any challenges minimised.

I suggest at this point you undertake both parts of the exercise in Toolkit Exercise 10 in Part 5 of the book. This exercise will help you to identify those areas of hypersensitivity that affect you individually. Even if you do not specifically suffer from hypersensitivity issues to your knowledge, the exercise could assist you in considering some of the environmental issues of choosing your own office space in general.

Once you have completed the exercise, the following section will provide some suggestions about things you need to ensure you take into account in choosing an office for your business.

Key considerations in choosing your office space

Toolkit Exercise 10 would have given you some more focused insight into those areas that are important for you in terms of hypersensitivities and challenges. I always say to people that I am not trying to highlight their differences or shortcomings when I go through an exercise such as this, but am instead trying to help people be aware of any areas that they need to take into account as being part of their make-up so that they can be accommodated in any decisions.

Let's have a look at some of the most important considerations relative to sensitivities.

Actual office layout

Make certain that the office space you rent or purchase is conducive to your needs. If you are the type of person who needs to be able to get away from the group relatively quickly (as in the case study above) make certain that you do not have to make your way through rows of open plan desks before you can get out. If you find that you need to avoid fluorescent lights when you are having an overload, make certain that the office does not have long corridors with no natural lighting and only fluorescent lighting. Even if you have an excellent office with good lighting, if there is a problem getting to and from that space, it doesn't really help.

Breakaway areas

This is something that most people do actually think about already. All that I would remind you to consider is the actual format of the breakaway areas. If they are noisy, overly bright or have distracting smells, then they really will not help at all. Also do you need to book them or are they freely available to use?

Other businesses in the area

Spend some time investigating the businesses that operate in the close vicinity of your office. There is nothing worse than signing the lease on office space only to discover in your first week that there is a factory nearby that has constant machinery running, or a hospital where ambulances are regularly travelling past with their sirens screaming. You may also want to be aware of whether there are things like schools in the area, especially if you are uncomfortable with crowds.

Other businesses sharing your floor in the building

Many office spaces require that you share an office block floor with other businesses. If this is the case with the office space you are looking to hire, do take the time to find out about the other companies on your level. It can be highly stressful to share the equivalent of an office space with a PR or communications company if you prefer to work in a more peaceful environment. Take time to visit the proposed office space so that you can see the shared space – is there a shared reception area? Do very energetic or loud people from other companies use the same space you need to?

Facilities

Other practicalities for you include the considerations around parking, public transport and/or car hire facilities. Do you need to have an office that has dedicated parking? Do you need to be near public transport links? Also think about things like the proximity of shops that you can buy supplies from such as coffee, tea, milk and sugar, as well as where you and your staff can get lunch. If the building has a canteen, does it look like it may be too loud or open for you to use? If you don't think you could use it comfortably, are there other places nearby to buy a sandwich? Or are there coffee areas in your office space that have microwave ovens? If there are – make sure these are not potentially near your office. Microwave buzzing and pinging can also be incredibly distracting!

Think about air conditioning. Are you affected by it? If you are not sure, try to spend some time in an air-conditioned office. Make sure that you have the ability to request the filters be cleaned if necessary.

Amenities

Now, this may be a very uncomfortable one to think about, but it is definitely an important one. Does the office have toilets and washrooms that suit your needs? I am the first to say that I really struggle to make use of a bathroom in an office building that only has one or two toilets. I also struggle to use public toilets where the cubicles are not properly 'enclosed' but have separating partitions that only come to your ankles rather than to the floor itself. Examine the toilets and make certain that you would actually be comfortable using them during the day.

Office equipment

If you are renting a furnished office, do make certain that they have the sort of equipment, desks and storage that you need. Generally, you would be getting you own computer equipment, so that would not be a problem, but you would probably be relying on them to provide you with operational printers and photocopier. Make certain that they do have the sort of equipment you would expect, and that there are enough of them. You do not want to be queuing to print out your client presentations with six people from other businesses ahead of you.

Also, make certain that you are happy with things like chairs and desks. You will always have the option of bringing in your own chairs if you have a special requirement that the company cannot meet, but desks are another matter.

Security

Last, think about the security arrangements of the building. If you are likely to be working late or unusual hours (as those of us on the spectrum are prone to do), you need to ensure that there will be no issues with you actually accessing the building, or that there is no risk to you as an individual due to security not being available after a certain time. Also make sure you are aware of what time car parks close (especially if they lock up) so that you know when to move your car if appropriate.

Having your own offices for the first time can be both exciting and challenging. Overall, I believe it is a wonderful experience to set up and establish your formal company office – provided you know in advance what to look for, what to avoid and how best to utilise what you have.

Chapter 18

Taking on other Shareholders

The Challenge of Sharing your Business

Many individuals with Asperger's make the decision to become entrepreneurs due to the appeal of working for oneself without the on-going challenge of dealing with others in the workplace, or having to report to someone. However, the reality is that as your business grows, you are going to have to bring other people in to work with you – either as employees, shareholders or partners in your business. We have already spoken about effectively employing and working with people in your business in Chapter 14, but in this chapter we are going to focus on what is perhaps more challenging for those of us with Asperger's, and that is sharing the business with other people.

I have previously emphasised that two of our major strengths as entrepreneurs are our tenacity and dedication which we end up applying to our new businesses. Once we have given ourselves a vision for our new area of focus, it does tend to become the centre of our lives (as we have discussed). Even if we ensure that we do not allow the new business to become our lives in totality, it is fair to say that that it will continue to be very focal and core to our existence going forward. This is our creation, our development – our 'baby' – and keeping to the analogy of it being our baby, it is fair to say that we will do everything we can to ensure that it is successful and provide for all its 'needs'.

As the business continues to grow and prosper, the time will generally arrive when you need to make the decision to bring other people into the business – not as employees, but as investors. There are two types of investment here – shareholders who invest money into your company in return for shares and dividend payments, and partners who invest money into the business in return for a share of the ownership and control of the business.

Reasons to consider the introduction of shareholders

There are a number of reasons to consider bringing in shareholders or other stakeholders. The most obvious of these is the fact that shareholders bring capital, or money, into the business. In the majority of cases, this is the main reason for considering the introduction of shareholders. In order to grow, your company will need additional funds that they can put towards expansion costs. Introducing shareholders into the business is one way of getting the funds without having to get bank loans or any other form of credit.

Another reason shareholders are introduced relates to the image or status of the company. A company is always seen as more credible where there is more than one director, or where there are a number of shareholders. Why? Well, it is largely to do with control and accountability. If there is only one key decision maker, this means that there will never be any formal challenge to that director's decisions or actions. Even if staff question the decisions of their manager or company director, they are not in a position to stop him or her actually taking those decisions. Another reasons is that – if high profile shareholders join or take interest in the company – this helps to put the business on the map due to the visibility of those people.

A third reason is in order to introduce key skills into the business. If there is a particular area of entrepreneurial business leadership that you really struggle with (such as sales, business development or marketing), you can bring in a partner who is very strong in these areas to be the lead for this. In entrepreneurial business development, it is not good practice for you to try to assign this to an employee. Generally, clients investing in a new business want to meet with a director of the company, and hence it would be better to bring someone into the business who is a partner or director.

OK, so we have spoken about some of the pros of introducing shareholders. So what are some of the challenges of introducing shareholders for those of us on the spectrum?

Asperger challenges of introducing other shareholders

The thought of 'outsiders' coming into our business tends to be something we – as entrepreneurs on the autism spectrum – do recognise as a part of business but do not necessarily pay that much attention to. After all, this *is* our business and most of us want to keep it to ourselves. I am certain that most of us on the autism spectrum will concede that we like to own our projects – sometimes to the point of possessiveness! Add to that the fact that most of us feel challenged by working relationships, and this will explain why we tend to prefer working alone or only with a small number of people we feel we can trust.

People interviewed as part of the book almost unanimously felt that one of our strengths as people on the autism spectrum is that we are able to work well alone and independently. I tend to agree. However, this reflects another sentiment in most cases – and this is that we *prefer* to work alone and independently. Let me share with you some of the comments made by our contributors:

'I think a few things make those on the spectrum more suited to entrepreneurial paths. 1) wanting things our own way, having our own schedule, without the need to conform, 2) challenging the status quo in actions and thoughts.' (Alex, entrepreneur)

'Being your own boss means that you can do things your way, even if it's unorthodox.' (Don Coulter)

'We work better by ourselves than as an employee or in a team environment. We are also born leaders. We see things from a different viewpoint, a viewpoint that most people don't have.' (Alison Bruning)

'The ability to work alone and make solo decisions is important. You never see this advertised for in corporate jobs. You can be yourself more – no cookie-cutter personalities, dress-codes and working styles.' (Gwyneth, entrepreneur)

This is summed up rather nicely by an additional comment from Alex, 'The desire to do things "our way" can be a double-edged sword, especially if one hasn't learned coping techniques or the basic social skills to conduct business professionally. To be one's "own boss" requires discipline, doing things one doesn't want to do, and to adapt to change when needed.'

Areas to be aware of in sharing your business

There are a few points I would like to highlight for anyone looking to introduce any shareholder into the business, more specifically those who make a contribution to the business as a whole, such as partners or directors.

Ensure a formal contract agreed with your lawyer

If you are going to be sharing part of your business with someone else, it is essential that you have this formalised in a contract that has been developed by a professional. Many people feel that this is not necessary, especially if the people concerned are family or friends. However, I would argue that this absolutely is necessary – *especially* if the people are family or friends.

It is extremely easy for your relationship as a friend or family member to influence your business decisions, and making the relationship more formal with a contract helps you to keep the focus of the relationship a business one.

In addition, this does help you to set boundaries where necessary in respect of what I refer to as family and friend exceptions. These are exceptions to our business thinking and standards that we allow for our family and friends, purely due to them being so close to us. So, for example, we could end up lending money to someone who is a family member, whereas we would not consider that if the person concerned wasn't related to us. This is not to say that this will also happen, but it certainly may. For people on the spectrum, the majority of us will go out of our way to assist someone we care about, sometimes to our own detriment. The role of the contract in this case is as much for our benefit as the other shareholder.

Be aware of oversensitivity to criticism or other inputs

One area that will be tested for you as a person on the spectrum when you bring in shareholders (if this is an area of sensitivity for you) is in the area of receiving criticism or other feedback. In general, most people (not only people on the spectrum) handle criticism in a number of ways:

1. They listen to the criticism, filtering relevant criticism from irrelevant criticism, discarding irrelevant criticism and acting on relevant criticism.

2. They listen to the criticism and act on everything, whether it is valid or not.

3. They listen to the criticism and take it to be a personal reflection on their short-comings.

4. They refuse to listen to the criticism and go on the defensive, having perceived the criticism as a personal attack.

For those of us on the spectrum, I would add that there are two additional ways we could react:

5. We get annoyed and intolerant with people who offer constructive feedback purely because they are challenging our way of doing things.

6. We hear the criticism, but ignore it as irrelevant, because we feel no-one could understand our business as well as we do.

An entrepreneur's response to criticism or feedback should ultimately be that detailed in point 1 above. However, we all know that this is particularly hard to do and that the reactions 3 through 6 are more likely to be what occurs.

When you have other people joining you in your business, part of what you should be expecting them to do is to give feedback on the business and how it is being operated and run. This feedback can sometimes include criticism. Learn to distinguish what is constructive criticism from what is malicious or irrelevant criticism. Malicious or irrelevant criticism is never acceptable from a business shareholder, and if you find that this is happening, you need to ensure that it is communicated to that shareholder that what they are doing is unacceptable. However, do make sure that you are properly interpreting their criticism, and whether or not it is relevant. There are a number of good books on the market that cover this topic in a lot of detail – far more than I can condense into this chapter – and if this is a challenging area for you, I do advise that you invest some time on this. I would recommend *Resilience: Facing Down Rejection and Criticism on the Road to Success* by Mark McGuinness (2013).

Be prepared to share!

Frequently, we make the decision to bring additional people into the business at a partner or director level, and then create problems by being unable to share the business with them. We have already said that people on the spectrum can be some of the most loyal and dedicated people you will find. However, with that dedication comes ownership. We really struggle to let go of something once we have taken the time start it up. I recommend that before you formalise an agreement with a partner or director you sit down and formally discuss their level of input in the organisation and come to an agreement. The final decision in that respect should be included in the contract discussed above.

Chapter 19

Learning to Live with Change

The Life of an Entrepreneur

Starting a career as an entrepreneur can be exciting and very fulfilling. However, for many people on the autism spectrum, there is another challenge to face that they do not foresee. The challenge is change.

An entrepreneurial world is a changing world

If you are making the move into your own business or have already done so, it is really important for you to understand that life as an entrepreneur strongly encompasses change. Being an employee – or even a leader – within a corporate environment, one often has the opportunity to develop and maintain regular or routine ways of working, or to establish set patterns such as taking a certain route to work in the morning, catching a specific time of train or bus, and so forth.

When we are entrepreneurs, this regularity disappears. Although it is fair to say that there will be certain parts of your entrepreneurial career that are still relatively regular or routine, the majority of it will change to be more variable. Some people can find this unsettling and unexpected, and do not cope very well with it. Let's discuss a couple of examples.

Potential challenges in maintaining routines

A large number of people on the autism spectrum (myself included!) find comfort and a sense of order through the development and maintenance of routines. We like to complete things a certain way, in a certain order, to a certain standard. I know that I still find great fulfilment in ordering my emails and electronic files in a particular way every day (a habit I regularly need to keep under control!).

As an entrepreneur, you may think that this wouldn't represent any kind of issue – after all, you are building your business around yourself. However, the reality is that small or new businesses are constantly adapting and changing. Together with this adaptation, developing established routines and fixed ways of working can be extremely challenging, and sometimes they can even be detrimental to the business itself. You are therefore likely to find that as soon as you have established a pattern of working that becomes your comfortable routine, you will find that this routine needs to change. For many people on the spectrum, this can end up being extremely stressful.

Learning to deal with constantly changing clients and staff

Another particularly relevant area of change relates to the changes you will experience with staff and clients. As a small business that is growing, you will be starting to take on employees as you expand your client base. Working in a corporate environment, we generally have the opportunity to get to know the people who work with and for us, since turnover in a corporate environment tends to be relatively low. However, in a start-up company, it is a fact of business that you can expect people to be joining and leaving the business a lot more than you may perhaps have been used to.

Building working relationships takes time for those of us on the spectrum, and it is something that we have to work at. As a result, it takes energy and concentration. Staff movements (both into and out of) your business will create tension for you just due to the nature of the way we need to deal with them, and hence it is always a good idea for you to ensure that you are expecting this and have sufficient energy reserves to cope.

However, it also means that we will need to adapt the way we go about building those relationships in the first place. As mentioned earlier in the book, the nature of building working relationships changes as an entrepreneur – you just do not have the time to spend building working relationships over a long period of time. You need to build them rapidly so that you work together effectively early on, and you also need to ensure that you have a release mechanism whereby you can accept that people are going to move on without feeling that this is a reflection on you or your business – it is just an inevitable part of being a start-up.

This leads to the situation with clients. Depending on the nature of your role in a corporate environment, we frequently have no direct dealings with clients, although of course we do have clients within the business. For those of you coming from this environment, moving to one where you are dealing with new clients on a regular basis can become overwhelming. Again, you need to work hard to establish a client relationship as part of your business development and customer relations' processes, but since there are generally clients leaving and new clients coming in on a regular basis, once again the relationship building becomes an on-going requirement.

'Well,' you may counter, 'this doesn't affect me because I dealt directly with customers in my corporate job so I am used to it.' Well, I would say that while this certainly will make things easier, it doesn't completely take away the change element. In reality, within a corporate environment, the organisation you are employed by is actually your greatest client. Therefore, despite the fact that you may be dealing with a number of clients and their resultant movements, you have the continuity and security of your employer as your key client. In an entrepreneurial business of your own, you are your own employer and therefore this does not apply.

Adaptive planning and operating

This is an area that it is important to understand as an entrepreneur. Whereas in the corporate world we will have learnt to develop very formal ways of structuring our business plans and following them through, and a set of operating procedures that we ensure are followed, as a start-up we cannot set such rigid ways of working. In fact, if we try to set formal structures and operating structures, these frequently interfere with the business in such a way as to result in the business failing to develop, a topic that was discussed earlier in the book.

Therefore, as an entrepreneur you are expected to be far more flexible in your planning and the way you work. Plans that you set up last month are going to change the following month to take into account developments and learning that has taken place during that time. Similarly, the way you work and the processes you follow may be revised as more optimal ways of working develop and people joining the business provide input. This whole process is known as *adaptive planning and operating*.

For people who find a sense of reassurance in unchanging systems or routines, this can be the most significant change challenge, as they end up clinging to the old ways of doing things without realising it. This can interfere with the growth of the business as well as potentially cause frustration to your team.

Growth is synonymous with change

It may seem an obvious comment that growth is synonymous with change, but we need to realise that our start-up organisations will be growing for many, many years to come – if not in size, then in the area of products, service levels, and so forth. Growth does not just mean the expansion of the business in terms of head count. It also includes the expansion of products, expertise, knowledge, sector credibility, and so forth.

As a person on the spectrum you need to understand that your life as an entrepreneur will centre on change far more than you may have been used to, and therefore your coping strategies for handling change will be far more important. It is also important that you understand how you may start to react to change so that you can be alert to the signals.

How do people on the autism spectrum generally react to stress?

This is a highly personal and individually variable topic. The way stress affects one person on the spectrum could differ considerably from the way it affects another. However, what I am looking at in this section are some of the generic causes for any challenges we may experience. Remember that the degree to which these apply to you depends on how well you currently cope with stress, how much exposure you have had to it in the past, and some of your individual sensory and cognitive challenges/strengths.

Sensory overload

Most of us with ASD have one or more hypersensitivities. For anyone who is not aware of what this is, this means that we have one or more overly sensitive perceptive senses, be it hearing, eyesight, smell, touch or taste, which are subject to overload due to too much input (Attwood 2007). Unlike neurotypicals, when we start to receive too much input to one of our hypersensitive senses, this creates the build-up of tension ultimately ending in an overload experience. When I first tried to understand how this differed from neurotypicals, the one thing that I realised after speaking to people was than for a neurotypical, removing oneself from an environment that was uncomfortable resulted in the discomfort immediately ceasing. For example, if someone turned on the radio and it was playing painfully loud, all they needed to do was turn the volume down and then things would be back to normal. We are generally not so fortunate. Let's take the same example. We turn on a radio and the volume is painfully loud. We immediately turn off the radio, but the pain and sensation of those voluminous sound waves continue to resound through us for an hour before they finally dissipate.

It is during this period of time when we cannot 'escape' from the effects of the excessive input that we tend to experience sensory overload. Effects of sensory overload differ per individual, but can include things such as headaches, panic attacks, inability to speak, inability to communicate, emotional outbursts and even the activation of co-morbid (or co-existing) conditions, such as epilepsy or asthma.

Need for time alone

As a result of the sensory overload issues discussed, we often need periods of time alone to recuperate. Coping with overloads or even just the business as usual coping strategies takes a lot of effort, and we require time apart from others to recover our energies. In a period of stress, this need for personal time increases as it takes longer for us to recover.

Hypervigilance

It is not surprising that people who have hypersensitivities tend to experience hypervigilance. This is when we are acutely aware of our surroundings and constantly on a lookout for things that can be perceived as threats, especially when we have recently had an overload experience. For example, someone with visual hypersensitivity could have experienced a recent overload due to working in an office with a faulty overhead light. The next week at work, that same individual is likely to be overly tense and observant regarding anything to do with the lights or visual stimuli.

Loss of focus

I find it interesting to read about the concept of what is termed monotropism (Murray, Lester and Lawson 2005). Monotropism is where we pay attention to or perceive detail, but struggle with seeing the big picture or whole. Attwood (2007) refers to this as weak central cohesion. My belief about entrepreneurs with Asperger syndrome is that we have been able to develop strategies to redress this shortfall quite early in our school careers, and that we have quite adept central coherence by the time we start our careers. I would be the last to say that we do not still have the propensity to get stuck in the detail, as you would have seen from what I have been discussing in the book so far. However, it is an area we have of necessity worked hard to compensate for.

There is one example provided by Tony Attwood (2007), however, that I personally do not agree with. In discussing the subject of weak central cohesion, Attwood describes our attention to details as being similar to a person looking at the world through a rolled up piece of paper, hence not seeing a lot of information. I dare to counter that example. I believe that actually we tend to see a lot more detail than most people. Far from seeing only a restricted view through the rolled up paper, we see *everything*.

Let me give you my own example for this. Imagine a situation where a family is sitting in their lounge. Suddenly they hear an unusual noise outside. In the one scenario, the father asks his neurotypical son to have a look outside and tell them what he sees. The son goes to the window and feeds back that he sees nothing – he has perceived that everything looks normal. In the second scenario, the father asks his Asperger son to look outside and tell them what he sees. The son goes to the window and feeds back that he sees the following: it is sunny, there is a light breeze that is moving the leaves on the trees nearby, there is a squirrel on the pathway, there are a number of cumulus clouds developing, there is a small fly caught in a spider's web on the outside of the window, there is a pair of turtle doves on the bush nearby... We do not see part of the picture outside the window, we see *everything*. Where we have a challenge is actually determining what from that information is relevant and what isn't. In the above example, the neurotypical son had attuned to look for something out of the ordinary, and therefore filtered out anything irrelevant. The son with Asperger's was not able to do this effectively.

As we have grown, we have developed techniques to recognise what we need to focus on and what we need to ignore or put aside to process later. Unlike neurotypicals, we do not automatically filter information. It is something we need to learn to do. By the time we have reached high school, this is generally something we can do quite effectively in normal circumstances.

However, in situations of stress, we may find that we become more distracted by irrelevant information. In a way, we regress to a situation where we could be having a conversation with someone about a very important topic only to interrupt ourselves mid-sentence to comment on the colour of butterfly that just flew past, or the unusual hairstyle of a colleague passing by in the corridor outside the meeting room.

Shutdowns

Shutdowns can often occur as a result of sensory overload. As a means to cut out this overwhelming bombardment of information and sensory data, we teach ourselves to block out the world. We switch off or shutdown. Sometimes we do this by totally ceasing to function, by going into our room and staring into space. However, for most of us, one of the ways we do this is to become totally engrossed in something. At work, this could mean that we sit down in front of our computer and effectively shut out the rest of the office. We don't hear, see or feel anything other than the computer. We are in a bubble.

In times of stress, we may find that we are starting to do this more frequently. We end up distancing ourselves from others unintentionally, and can be seen to be ignoring the people around us.

Perfectionism

Many of us experience a level of personal perfectionism is areas where we believe we can do well. Our thinking tends to be black or white, and therefore we tend to see our own performance as either good or bad. As people with an ASD, we put a high value on the concept of intelligence. Generally, this is because we see it as an area we are not hindered by any developmental disorders, and have not had to struggle with as much as other areas such as social and communication skills. We obtain a lot of our sense of worth from our ability to perform well. Any perception on our part that we are under-performing can cause great frustration and stress for us.

So we have covered why it is important to understand how you react to change. Shall we examine the actual effects?

Order and routine

Almost everyone on the spectrum craves order and routine. By the time we have become professionals within business, we have learnt to find ways to ensure that this predisposition does not become an undue focus for us. However, when a situation becomes stressful, we can revert to needing order and routine around us. We can end up spending significant amounts of time ordering our desks, or categorising projects, or developing a new labelling technique for our calendars. Similarly, we may develop an increased tendency to rigidly adhere to the rules and established procedures during times of stress, far more than we ordinarily would. As mentioned earlier, this is exactly the opposite behaviour to what we require as an entrepreneur.

Stimming

Stimming (abbreviated from the word stimulating) is where we undertake some kind of repetitive physical activity aimed at focusing our attention away from a stressor and therefore bringing that stress under control. Examples of stimming would include rapid finger tapping, rapid toe or foot tapping, rocking, humming, finger or hand flapping or bouncing in one's seat. As with most things, stimming is highly individual. For those of us who have been in business for a long time, we have either learnt to suppress any stimming, or to convert to a type of stimming which is more socially acceptable. However, when a situation becomes stressful, it is highly likely that stimming may increase, or you may inadvertently revert to what you may consider your less favourable stimming methods.

Living with change is an essential element of becoming an entrepreneur, as I have emphasised throughout this chapter. However, it is certainly something that we can learn to do, and can learn to do very well. If you feel this is an area of particular challenge for you, I would like to suggest that you read my book, *An Asperger Leader's Guide to Living and Leading Change* (Bergemann 2013) since this contains a lot of exercises to help you make change more manageable.

Conclusion

The purpose of this book has been to cover the topic of entrepreneurship, looking at it through both neurotypical eyes and our own unique perspectives as individuals on the autism spectrum. Entrepreneurship provides the opportunity for many people on the autism spectrum to excel in a way they never would have been free to do had they remained in the corporate world. Still other people on the spectrum make the move from a highly successful corporate career into entrepreneurship in order to escape the on-going challenges they need to overcome in the corporate environment just to ensure they fit within a neurotypical world that frequently undervalues the unique strengths of the Asperger professional.

I hope that reading this book has encouraged you either to make the decision to enter the entrepreneurial world, or has provided you with some tools to optimise your experience of it if you are already there. Being an entrepreneur can be an incredibly rewarding experience that allows us to use and share those skills and talents that only we as people on the autism spectrum have. I hope that you are encouraged by the comments and experiences of some of the other entrepreneurs on the spectrum who have contributed to this book.

Always remember: Your uniqueness is what makes you who you are. Having an autism spectrum disorder is one of your unique qualities that carries with it a multitude of skills that are incredibly valuable to the entrepreneurial world. Go out and make your mark.

Part 5 contains a number of toolkits and exercises which are available to be downloaded from www.jkp.com/catalogue/book/9781849055093/resources.

PART 5

Practical Tools and Exercises

TOOLKIT EXERCISE 1
UNDERSTANDING YOUR MOTIVATION FOR STARTING A BUSINESS

In Chapter 2 we discussed some of the reasons people have for deciding to start their own businesses. As part of that discussion, we emphasised how important it was for you to understand your personal drivers for wanting to start you own company, in order that you ensure your business meets those needs and does not conflict with them in any way.

The following exercise will assist you in focusing on some of the essential considerations relevant to starting your own business. This isn't a long exercise, but it does encourage you to think about a number of elements of your work, your personality and your ambitions that you may not have considered before deciding to start your company. The exercise is divided into two parts: Part 1 will be asking you specific questions about some key areas and how you experience or feel about these. These questions are not intended to be too leading or closed, but to encourage you to think about the topic. There are no right or wrong answers, and not every area will have significance for you. Just ensure that before you mark an area as not applicable, you take some time to think about it – is it really non-applicable?

Part 2 of the exercise asks you to consider some of the implications of the exercise in Part 1, and how this could affect your decisions in starting your own business.

Part 1: Your individual profile

Instructions

The following tables include questions on some key areas. Read through the questions and spend some time thinking about whether each applies to you, and if so, how. Make sure you do take the time to make some notes on this, even if they are bullet points. These tables can be downloaded from www.jkp.com/catalogue/book/9781849055093/resources.

KEY QUESTIONS ON ENTREPRENEURIAL MOTIVATION

What is the main reason for you wanting to start your own business?

Have you experienced something in your corporate working environment that has made you uncomfortable or unhappy (e.g. bullying, politics, aggressive managers, etc.)?

How important is it for you to have control of your work and/or your work environment? Why is this?

How well do you work with other people? Is this a key reason for deciding to work for yourself?

cont.

What is the thing that you enjoy doing most as part of your work? Why?

What kinds of things create overload for you in the workplace?

How are you at business development or sales?

How are you at networking?

How are you with travelling?

What are your written communication skills like?

How are you when it comes to overload? Do you need to be isolated?
What are your coping strategies? How can it affect other people?

Have you been told that you are very direct or too truthful? If so,
how do you think this could be an issue (or not an issue) in your own
business?

cont.

Do you have sensory issues such as hyper- or hyposensitive hearing, sight, smell, etc.? How could this be a consideration in starting your business, or in what your intended line of business is?

Have you found that there are things in your life that may cause you to get depressed (e.g. people disagreeing with you, too much isolation, too much interaction with people)? If yes, do you think this could potentially arise in the context of your business?

Are there any other areas which you think are very important to you which you need to make sure that you either incorporate into your business, or ensure your business allows you to cater for (e.g. compulsory behaviours, stimming, need for a breakaway area, need to have a 'dark room')?

Have you already considered a backup or contingency plan for when you may not be available to your business (e.g. through illness, holiday, etc.)?

Part 2: Understanding your individual profile

Instructions

Following your answers to the questions in the previous section, the next table includes the same questions, but with some additional considerations for you. Read through each question again and spend some time thinking about whether this applies to you, and if so, how. Make sure you do take the time to make some notes on this, even if they are bullet points.

KEY QUESTIONS ON ENTREPRENEURIAL MOTIVATION

What is the main reason for you wanting to start your own business?
In answering this question this time, do you think that some of the questions in the previous section may make you change your reasons for starting your own business somewhat? Make sure that you think about it and make sure that there are no underlying reasons for starting your business that you hadn't considered. Consider whether the question about experiences in the corporate environment may change your view somewhat.
How important is it for you to have control of your work and/or your work environment? Why is this?
The way you answered this question may determine whether you start a business where clients have a lot of control over things such as your time, your methods, what you produce. It may also make you consider some things you need to ensure you retain control of so that you do not get frustrated. Make a note of some of these, or any considerations relating to this.

cont.

How well do you work with other people? Is this a key reason for deciding to work for yourself?

Again, this may well determine the type of business you want to start, or the structure of the business. Do you need to think about getting a people manager? Do you need some coaching on dealing with people? Could this create a problem with clients? Make a note of what you could do to ensure that this is taken account of in your new business so that things work optimally.

What is the thing that you enjoy doing most as part of your work? Why?

Are you certain that your business idea will not interfere with you still being able to do what you enjoy the most? That may not necessarily be a particular task, but thinking about why you enjoy a particular task may give you some insights into other areas that may be important for you. Are there any areas of your business idea you need to refine in the light of these considerations?

What kinds of things create overload for you in the workplace?

Have you taken into consideration that this may be an issue in your business? Are these areas either eliminated or a coping strategy developed? Make a note of some of the strategies you have for the things you have identified that could arise in your own business.

How are you at business development or sales?

After having answered this question, do you have to make any adjustments to your new business idea, such as bringing someone in to assist you in this area? Or is it an identified area of development for you? Make a note of how this will affect your business idea.

How are you at networking?

After having answered this question, do you have to make any adjustments to your new business idea, such as bringing someone in to coach you in this area? Is it an identified area of development for you? How important will the networking be? Can you make use of social media? Make a note of how this will affect your business idea.

How are you with travelling?

Many people on the spectrum struggle with travelling and changes of venue. If you are starting your own business, will you be required to travel to client sites or other offices? Do you have coping mechanisms for this? Make a note of how this will influence your planning for your business.

cont.

What are your written communication skills like?

Sometimes people on the spectrum can have challenges with written communication, sometimes misinterpreting implications or being too direct. Will you be required to have a lot of written communication with clients, suppliers or staff? Is this an area you could benefit with support such as a personal assistant? Make a note of how this could affect your business model.

How are you when it comes to overload? Do you need to be isolated? What are your coping strategies? How can it affect other people?

Have you thought about any areas of your potential business that could aggravate your overloads? If you have, make a note of how you can change your business plans to accommodate or avoid this.

Have you been told that you are very direct or too truthful? If so, how do you think this could be an issue (or not an issue) in your own business?

As with written communication, sometimes people on the spectrum can annoy neurotypicals by being too truthful, ironic as that seems. Will you be required to have a lot of verbal communication with clients, suppliers or staff? Is this an area you could benefit with support such as a personal assistant? Make a note of how this could affect your business model.

Do you have sensory issues such as hyper- or hyposensitive hearing, sight, smell, etc.? How could this be a consideration in starting your business, or in what your intended line of business is?
Have you considered how your business idea could affect you as far as your sensitivities go? If so, what are you going to have to do to ensure it does not become an issue? Make some notes here.

Have you found that there are things in your life that may cause you to get depressed (e.g. people disagreeing with you, too much isolation, too much interaction with people)? If yes, do you think this could potentially arise in the context of your business?
What can you do to ensure that this does not occur, or if it does, that you have a coping strategy? Make some notes here.

Are there any other areas that you think are very important to you that you need to make sure that you either incorporate into your business, or ensure your business allows you to cater for (e.g. compulsory behaviours, stimming, need for a breakaway area, need to have a 'dark room').
Having considered the above, think about the practicalities of how you can deal with or incorporate the areas you identified and make some notes.

cont.

Have you already considered a backup or contingency plan for when you may not be available to your business (e.g. through illness, holiday, etc.)?

Do make sure that you think about cover for you. Much as we like to think we are, we actually are not supposed to work 24/7 365 days a year. All of us need a break, and we need to make sure we have a plan for that which does not create undue stress or concerns for us when the time draws near. Make a note of any thoughts you have had about this.

TOOLKIT EXERCISE 2

AGREEING POLICIES AND PROCESSES

In Chapter 3 we discussed the challenge that people moving from a corporate career to a small business experience when it comes to setting up policies and procedures. We emphasised that it is very important to make certain that you do not make the error of trying to implement corporate policies into a small business that are totally inappropriate.

The following exercise will assist you in determining whether some of the policies and procedures you are considering implementing are actually relevant for a start-up or small business. I generally recommend that this is done as part of an early team meeting, giving your direct reports an opportunity to have an input.

Remember that the purpose of this activity is to obtain input from your team and overall agreement on the terms. Do not be afraid to hear objections to policies or processes that you feel are important, and be open to hearing them. I have sometimes been pleasantly surprised by the input of a team member who has given me a totally new outlook on a certain process.

Instructions

The table that follows, Exercise Table 2.1, is a template that allows you to list some of the policies and procedures that you are considering developing format documentation for. Circulate the spreadsheet to your team ahead of your scheduled meeting, asking them to start to populate the sheet with a list of policies and procedures you need to review. You should also complete your own version of the spreadsheet.

On the day of the meeting, take Exercise Table 2.2 with you to the meeting. On this document, you can – as you progress through the meeting – list all of the policies and procedures that have been listed by your team. Take the time then to consider each policy/procedure that has been listed to consider how many people this policy affects, whether it is a legal requirement, whether it is business critical and whether following this policy/procedure will be restrictive to staff or managers. Finally, based on this discussion, make the decision whether or not to introduce the policy and who will be responsible for it.

Exercise Table 2.1

Name of policies or procedures to discuss and agree

Exercise Table 2.2

How many people will this affect in the business?	Is this required by law? If yes, which one?	Is this policy/ procedure business critical?	Could this negatively impact on staff or managers? If yes, how?	Introduce the policy/ process?	Owner	Name of policy or procedure

TOOLKIT EXERCISE 3

KEY SYSTEMS, DEPARTMENTS AND PEOPLE

In Chapter 4 we challenged you to think about some of the systems and departments that are appropriate for a small or start-up business as opposed to a corporate business. In order to assist you in doing this, we have provided you with a basic template to use as part of your analysis.

Instructions

Spend some time completing the following template, Exercise Table 3.1, considering as many of the corporate policies and procedures you can think of or have experienced.

Exercise Table 3.1

Function, department or system	In what way can you use this in your small business?	Is this an essential or a nice to have?

UNDERSTANDING YOUR FINANCIAL REQUIREMENTS

In Chapter 5 we discussed some of the things you need to consider in order to ascertain whether or not you are ready to start your own business at this stage in your life and career. What follows are a series of exercises as highlighted in Chapter 5 of the book. Note that most of these relate to the table that follows. It is intended that you update your table as appropriate as part of each exercise, and therefore only one copy of the table is printed. However, if you would like to have additional copies of these to work with, you can download copies from www.jkp.com/catalogue/book/9781849055093.

EXERCISE 4.1

YOUR INITIAL THOUGHTS ON RESOURCES

Complete Exercise Table 4.1 on the following page, thinking about your current financial situation. If you are currently employed and are considering making the move to your own business, complete column 2, followed by column 3 – as directed in Chapter 5. If you are currently working in your own business, start from column 3, as directed in Chapter 5.

Exercise Table 4.1

	1	2	3	4
	In your current job	As a start-up: first thoughts	As a start-up: thoughts after considering time	As a start-up: thoughts after considering knowledge
Personal				
Your pay (net)				
Spouse's pay (net)				
Other income				
Total Personal Income				
Mortgage/rent				
Vehicle costs				
Fuel				
Other transport costs				
Utilities				
Rates and taxes				
Telephone				
Internet				
Food and groceries				
Pet costs				
Insurances				
Clothes				
School fees				
Birthdays/holidays				
Entertainment				

	1	2	3	4
	In your current job	**As a start-up: first thoughts**	**As a start-up: thoughts after considering time**	**As a start-up: thoughts after considering knowledge**
Hobbies				
Gym				
Medical				
Credit cards and accounts				
Others				
1				
2				
3				
Total Personal Expenses				
Business				
Revenue (gross)	N/A			
Other business income	N/A			
Total Business Income				
Company taxes	N/A			
Office rental	N/A			
Company vehicle costs	N/A			
Company vehicle fuel	N/A			
Other transport costs	N/A			
Office furniture rental	N/A			
Computer equipment	N/A			
Office utility costs	N/A			
Office rates and taxes	N/A			
Telephones	N/A			
Internet	N/A			
IT software	N/A			
Marketing costs	N/A			
Advertising costs	N/A			

cont.

	1 In your current job	2 As a start-up: first thoughts	3 As a start-up: thoughts after considering time	4 As a start-up: thoughts after considering knowledge
Insurances	N/A			
Salaries	N/A			
Employee benefits costs	N/A			
Other staff costs	N/A			
Stock	N/A			
Production costs	N/A			
Stationery costs	N/A			
Postage and printing costs	N/A			
Subscriptions/ professional membership	N/A			
Other operational costs	N/A			
1	N/A			
2	N/A			
3	N/A			
Total Business Expenses				
Personal And Business				
Total Income (Personal + Business) (A)				
Total Expenditure (Personal + Business) (B)				
Profit/Reserves (A-B)				

EXERCISE 4.2

A REVIEW OF YOUR TIME COMMITMENTS

When asked to consider how much time we have available for a new project or for work, we can terribly underestimate the amount of time we have available to us, and as a result can end up making commitments that we actually cannot honour – purely because we run out of time. In this exercise, we aim to get a more realistic record of how much time you have available to you currently, as well as how much time you would have available to you should you decide to start your own business.

In this exercise, we ask you to commit at least one week of your time recording your actual activities in the table below. If you are able to do two weeks – even better! Just download a second copy of the template. This table will record how you are currently spending your time. Make sure that you try to record this as accurately as possible. To make the process easier, we have suggested that you use codes or abbreviations for certain key activities, and you have been provided with a key table that you can use to record things relevant to you. We have started to populate this with some relevant ones to assist you.

There is one thing to keep in mind. Although it is true that many of us on the autism spectrum find that we actually seem to have less of a requirement for sleep than neurotypicals, do make sure that you are realistic with your sleep time allocation. Once you start your own business, there is the possibility that things may initially be challenging for you, resulting in overload issues at some point. You would then need to ensure that you have 'budgeted' sufficient recovery time in the form of sleep or downtime.

Start to complete Exercise Table 4.2 now, and return to this exercise once you have recorded a week's worth of time usage.

Abbreviations for Exercise Table 4.2

Sleep	SL	Reading	RT
Eating	EA	Alone time	AT
Study time	ST	Travel time	TT
Family time	FT	Others	
Examinations	EX		
Research time	RT		
Bathing/ showers	BS		

Exercise Table 4.2 Weekly Time Analysis

	Monday	Tuesday	Wednesday	Thursday	Friday	Saturday	Sunday
00:00							
01:00							
02:00							
03:00							
04:00							
05:00							
06:00							
07:00							
08:00							
09:00							
10:00							
11:00							
12:00							
13:00							
14:00							
15:00							
16:00							
17:00							
18:00							
19:00							
20:00							
21:00							
22:00							
23:00							

Now that you have completed Exercise 4.2, you should have a better idea of the sort of time commitments and availability you have. It is important to remember that this is currently an estimate of your time, not a rigid pattern, but it will give you an idea of where any opportunities for investing time may lie.

EXERCISE 4.3

REVIEWING YOU INITIAL THOUGHTS AFTER CONSIDERING TIME

Now that you have considered what time resources you have, you need to update your original financial sheet to take into account any changes made by your time commitment considerations. Examples of changes could include reducing your business revenue for the month because you have realised you do not have as much time to spend with clients, or introducing some staff costs because you realised you do not have time to be in your business as much as you need to be, or do not have holiday cover.

Update column 4 of Exercise Table 4.1 at the beginning of the toolkit, after having thought about the implications of time considerations from Exercise 4.2.

EXERCISE 4.4

CONSIDERING GAPS IN YOUR KNOWLEDGE

Now that you have considered finances and time, you need to start thinking about your third resource, and that is knowledge. When we speak about knowledge as a resource, there are really two elements we are considering. The first is the knowledge required *by you* as the entrepreneur in starting up your business, and the second is the knowledge required *within your business* as a whole in order for it to be a successful entity.

Let's start by looking at the first of these knowledge points – you. We can do this by asking three key questions:

1. What knowledge do you personally need in order to become a successful entrepreneur?

2. Do you have any gaps in your knowledge in the sector or specialist area you want to start your business?

3. If there are any gaps identified under 1. or 2., do they need to be filled by you personally?

The first question is quite a broad one, and sometimes people spend quite a lot of time thinking about this, ending up still uncertain as to the answer. I would suggest that in considering this question, it is worthwhile thinking about the sorts of activities that need to take place within your business: finance, developing a website, customer services, business development, networking, public speaking, drawing up contracts for clients, and so forth. This is actually covered under the second of these knowledge points, namely the knowledge required in your business as a whole.

To help you organise your thoughts in this area, this exercise provides you with another template to complete. This template asks you to list the key activities in your business, as outlined above, as well as the key knowledge areas for your specialist area or sector. It then invites you to consider whether each of these is knowledge required by you personally or required within the business, and then to consider whether the knowledge is there or not. Finally, it asks you to think about what steps need to be taken to fill any identified gaps.

Complete the template now to give some thought to some of the key areas of knowledge that you will require in running your own business and whether or not these skills currently exist either with you or within your business. Next decide on how you are going to address any gaps.

Exercise Table 4.4

What knowledge do you and your business need to be successful in your market? *Include the following considerations: technical; sector; business-related; personal*	Do you have this knowledge?	Do you need to have this personally?	Does someone in your business have this knowledge?	Is it a gap?	If so, how will you fill it?

REVIEWING YOUR INITIAL THOUGHTS AFTER CONSIDERING KNOWLEDGE

Exercise 4.4 should have helped you to determine whether there are areas relevant to knowledge that will require some time and finance commitments from you. For example, you may well have identified that you need to be familiar with at least the basics of book-keeping, and therefore that you need to enrol in a book-keeping course, which has cost and time implications. Another example could be that you identify that you need web design skills in the business and you decide this is something you will address by hiring someone.

Now, as a final step, you will need to revise your original financial forecast taking into account the results of your work in Exercise 4.4. To this by updating column 4 of the table at the beginning of the toolkit, after having thought about the implications of knowledge as directed in Exercise 4.4.

TOOLKIT EXERCISE 5
YOUR START-UP CHECKLIST

In Chapter 5 we discussed some of the things you need to think about in starting your business. What follows is a start-up checklist which details some of the most essential things that you need to consider before actually starting up your business.

Take some time now to review the list and note where you are in the process. As you progress through the book, you can then make more notes on what your thoughts are.

Note that some of these questions are not specifically addressed through this book, questions such as 'How do I register my company?' and 'How do I register my company name?' The reason for this is that every country has different legal requirements and points of contact in this respect. An internet search should provide you with relevant details for your country.

Exercise Table 5.1

	I haven't considered it yet	I am thinking about it	I have made a decision	Notes/Final Decision
What type of business structure will suit my business best?				
What are the legal requirements associated with registering my company?				
Do I need to register for tax, and how do I do this?				
What business name should I use and how do I register it?				

What sort of insurance do I need to obtain for myself and my business (e.g. professional indemnity, employer liability)			
Where should my office be based? Should it be a formal office or a virtual environment?			
What will be my staffing requirements? Will these be full-time or part-time posts? How do I go about recruiting them?			
Am I going to use an internal accounting and payroll system or am I going to outsource it? If so, what are the costs?			

TOOLKIT EXERCISE 6

YOUR INITIAL BUDGET

Now that you have decided to start your own business, it is important for you to develop your first budget. As discussed in Chapter 6, what follows is an elementary budget sheet for you to use, covering four periods. If you are just starting your business, I recommend that the periods concerned are actually months. This allows you to get used to budgeting and to see how accurate you are with your forecasting of costs and income.

Remember that in terms of income, you should only record sales receipts that you actually receive. Therefore, if you have invoiced £20,000 but have only been paid £5000 so far, you enter £5000 as your sales receipts, not £20,000.

Similarly, if you receive an invoice that you do not pay for this month, you do not enter the value of the invoice in this month, but only record this when it is actually paid.

Exercise Table 6.1 Cash Flow Budget

	Period 1	**Period 2**	**Period 3**	**Period 4**
Opening Balance	0	Closing balance from Period 1	Closing balance from Period 2	Closing balance from Period 3
Cash Income				
Sales receipts				
Other income				
Other income				
Total Cash Income	Add all income figures	Add all income figures	Add all income figures	Add all income figures
Cash Outgoings				
Purchase of equipment				
Purchases of inventory				
Salaries and wages				

	Period 1	Period 2	Period 3	Period 4
Human resources costs				
Water and electricity				
Telephones				
IT costs				
Rent and rates				
Cleaning and repairs				
Marketing				
Printing and stationery				
Software				
PC/printer consumables				
Website costs				
Other office costs				
Post and packaging				
Insurance				
Vehicle costs				
Fuel				
Other travel costs				
Accommodation costs				
Subsistence				
Mileage payments				
Parking costs				
Advertising				
Legal fees				
Accountants fees				
Bank charges				

cont.

	Period 1	Period 2	Period 3	Period 4
Interest payable				
Contingency amount				
Others				
Total Cash Outgoings	Add all outgoing figures	Add all outgoing figures	Add all outgoing figures	Add all outgoing figures
Closing Balance	Opening Balance + Total Cash Income: Cash Outgoing	Opening Balance + Total Cash Income: Cash Outgoing	Opening Balance + Total Cash Income: Cash Outgoing	Opening Balance + Total Cash Income: Cash Outgoing

TOOLKIT EXERCISE 7

SAMPLE INVITATION TO TENDER DOCUMENT

From: xxx [the company]

Address

To: xxx [the tenderer]

INVITATION TO TENDER/REQUEST FOR PROPOSAL –

CONTRACT NUMBER [insert contract reference]

1. You are invited by the [company], to submit a tender for [insert title].

2. This ITT/RFP is confidential and proprietary to [company]. The material contained within it shall be treated as confidential by potential suppliers. The potential supplier shall use the information only for the purpose of preparing a response to this ITT. The information may not be used or shared with other parties for any purpose without [company's] prior consent.

3. Please read all the documents listed in the Form of Tender. Should your tender be accepted, these documents, your tender and any changes agreed in writing will form a binding contract between you and [company].

4. The contract will be for a period of [insert number] [weeks/months/years], beginning on xx/xx/xxxx unless extended or terminated according to the enclosed Terms of Reference.

5. If you do not wish to submit a tender, please return this covering letter using the addressed label which should be clearly marked '*No Tender*'. If you can state your reasons for not tendering this would be useful and may help to inform us on future procurements.

6. One original and [insert number] copies (so marked) of your tender and proposals, including any covering letter, will be required.

7. Tenders must be *delivered BY 12.00 HOURS ON* [insert date]. The tender document should be addressed to myself at the above address. Late tenders will not be admitted and it is your responsibility to ensure that your tender is received.

8. Any subsequent contract, if awarded, will be subject to the enclosed Terms of Reference.

9. You can obtain further information about contractual issues from myself (The Procurement Officer) at the above address, or from [insert name] at [insert address and phone number] for technical matters.

Questions/clarifications on this ITT may be made before xx/xx/xx. The [Company] will summarise all the questions and responses and this will be made available to all potential suppliers.

Return procedure

1. Please respond to all requirements.

2. Please return the completed prices schedule [and Form of Tender].

3. Tenders shall take the following format: *Lay out any specific format for the tender response, to make the evaluation easier e.g. the tender response must follow the headings in the specification.*

Timetable summary

The Timetable is not binding and may be changed if circumstances so dictate.

Action	Date
Questions on ITT	
Return of tenders	
Notification to suppliers of evaluation	
Contract commencing	

Optional

Include either here, in the Specification or in a separate 'information required from you' sheet, any additional requirements for information such as:

- Details of any proposed sub-contractors, including reasons for selection.

- Details of QA systems.

- Business or professional references.

- A method statement, explaining how you propose to plan and carry out the work. This should include details of your Quality Assurance Systems and how they will be applied to this contract.

- List of named personnel including CVs.

- References, preferably for similar work, for both your organisation and any individuals proposed for the contract, including full name, job title, address and telephone number of referees.

- Details of all three current, similar, contracts.

Disclaimer

- The issuing of the ITT and any responses do not imply that [company] will enter into a contract or accept any proposal with any potential suppliers.

- The potential supplier is responsible for costs of any kind incurred in the response to this ITT.

- For goods: There is no guarantee of representation regarding the levels of business which [company] may place with a potential supplier. While [company] has used reasonable commercial endeavours in compiling this information, we do not warrant the accuracy of this information.

- By submitting a response to the ITT you are agreeing to be bound by the enclosed terms and conditions.

- The information set out in this ITT and accompanying documents has been compiled with care but does not necessarily represent with total accuracy the company's position and in the absence of fraud [company] shall have no liability in respect of the accuracy of any such information or any related representation or statement.

- The tenders shall be valid for a period of [number] months of the closing date of receipt of tenders.

Enclosed

- [Form of tender].
- Specification/Requirements.
- Standard Terms and Conditions of Supply.

TOOLKIT EXERCISE 8
NETWORKING FLOWCHART

Pre-event Preparation

- Acknowledge.
- Research: host, event, venue, others.
- Develop introduction.
- Develop conversation starters and reciprocal answers.
- Business cards.

Handling the Event

- Eye contact and facial expressions.
- Keep hands busy.
- Make introductions pleasant.
- Focus on people, not food.
- Brief conversations.
- Business cards as exit strategies.

Recharging

- Quiet space.
- Be aware of stressor and its termination point.
- Make brief notes of event.
- Have hobby on standby.

Follow-up

- Review notes.
- Email or write to appropriate people.
- Schedule a second follow-up.

NOTEPAD FOR RECORDING A NETWORK SESSION

In Chapter 15 I spoke about the need to make some notes about the people we have networked with, relatively soon after we have had the opportunity to speak to them. I find the following template useful in remembering the important information I need to recall about people, over and above their business card details. As I say, I suggest you do this shortly after the event, when details are still fresh in your mind.

Exercise Table 9.1

Networking summary form
Name of person
Organisation
Role in company
Contact details
How/where did I meet them *(i.e. did you meet during a coffee break, the dinner, were you seated together, etc.)*?

cont.

What did they look like?

What were some important things we discussed? *(Include important informal information.)*

Were there any positive impressions I gained?

Were there any negative impressions I gained?

Did we agree to follow-up formally or informally?

Do I want to follow-up?

Details of any follow-up

TOOLKIT EXERCISE 10

UNDERSTANDING YOUR POTENTIAL HYPERSENSITIVITIES

In Chapter 17 we started to discuss obtaining your own business space. As mentioned in the chapter, this is something that needs to be done after some particular consideration of how the office space you choose could affect you as an individual on the autism spectrum. Whether or not you are aware of having any sensory hypersensitivities, it is important that you take the time to think about what in your working environment could either optimise or hinder your performance as an individual, as well as affect how you work with your team.

The following exercise will assist you in focusing on some of the essential considerations relevant to choosing office space for you. The exercise is divided into two parts: Part 1 will be asking you specific questions about some key behaviours and whether or not you experienced these – either previously (such as at high school or in your early career) or currently. Part 2 of the exercise asks you to consider some work situations and determine how you would either be affected by these or would handle them.

Part 1: Your individual behaviours

Instructions

The following tables show some of the more common issues experienced by those of us on the autism spectrum and allows you to indicate the degree to which these were representative of your behaviour in the workplace.

Exercise Table 10.1

My key: Behavioural Indicators during Work	Does not apply	Mild or irregular	Quite often	Regularly	Almost all the time	Key problem area
Aggression/overly assertive						
Isolating oneself						
Anxiety						
Depression						
Tantrums/outbursts						
Inability or difficulty making friends						
Problems with teamwork						
Problems with conversations (inappropriate comments, speaking too fast/slow, interrupting others, going off topic)						
Rituals or compulsory behaviours						
Specialist interest being focal						
Difficulties understanding other people's thoughts or reactions (mindblindness)						
Sensory hypersensitivities						
Poor co-ordination and/or balance						
Stimming behaviour						
Problems interpreting instructions (taking things too literally)						
Very blunt/matter of fact with opinions						
Problems with personal body language (lack of or inappropriate facial expressions, gestures or actions, inappropriate stimming)						
Problems interpreting body language in others						
Problems with eye contact						
Problems with proximity/personal space						

Hypervigilance						
Inability to focus on a task due to distractions						
Getting too caught up in the details of an assignment without being able to see the overview (e.g. writing a detailed essay but not being able to summarise it appropriately)						
Perfectionism (struggling to leave tasks until they are perfect)						
Difficulty with verbal directions or instructions						
Dependent on instructions; not being proactive						
Insistence of doing things your way and no other						
Problems multi-tasking						
Problems delegating						
Sensory overload						
Shutdown or deliberate isolation						
Others (detail)						

Part 2: Early work experiences

Having thought about your key behavioural indicators and how you have managed them over time, spend some time thinking of coping strategies that would be appropriate for you to utilise should your behaviour regress in any particular area. In addition, think about how you would recognise if your behaviours were regressing. This will help you to be more aware if this actually starts happening in reaction to a change programme, and will allow you more time to adjust your coping strategies.

Exercise Table 10.2

My Current Key Behavioural Indicators	How will changes in this area manifest?	Proposed practical coping strategies
Aggression		
Isolating oneself		
Anxiety		
Depression		

Tantrums/outbursts		
Inability or difficulty making friends		
Problems with teamwork		
Problems with conversations (inappropriate comments, speaking too fast/slow, interrupting others, going off topic)		
Rituals or compulsory behaviours		

My Current Key Behavioural Indicators	How will changes in this area manifest?	Proposed practical coping strategies
Specialist interest being focal		
Difficulties understanding other people's thoughts or reactions (mindblindness)		
Sensory hypersensitivities		
Poor co-ordination and/or balance		
Stimming behaviour		

Problems interpreting instructions (taking things too literally)			
Very blunt/matter of fact with opinions			
Problems with personal body language (lack of or inappropriate facial expressions, gestures or actions, inappropriate stimming)			
Problems interpreting body language in others			
Hypervigilance			

cont.

My Current Key Behavioural Indicators	How will changes in this area manifest?	Proposed practical coping strategies
Problems with eye contact		
Problems with proximity/personal space		
Inability to focus on a task due to distractions		
Getting too caught up in the details of an assignment without being able to see the overview (e.g. writing a detailed essay but not being able to summarise it appropriately)		
Perfectionism (struggling to leave tasks until they are perfect)		

Difficulty with verbal directions or instructions		
Dependent on instructions; not being proactive		
Insistence of doing things your way and no other		
Problems multi-tasking		
Problems delegating		

cont.

My Current Key Behavioural Indicators	How will changes in this area manifest?	Proposed practical coping strategies
Sensory overload		
Shutdown or deliberate isolation		
Others (detail)		

References

Aldrich, H.E. and Widenmayer, G. (1993) 'From traits to rates: An ecological perspective on organizational foundings.' *Advances in Entrepreneurship, Firm Emergence and Growth 1*, 145–195.

American Psychiatric Association (2013), *Diagnostic and Statistical Manual of Mental Disorders, Fifth Edition (DSM-5)*. Washington DC: American Psychiatric Publishing.

Attwood, T. (2007) *The Complete Guide to Asperger's Syndrome*, London: Jessica Kingsley Publishers.

Bandura, A. (ed.) (1995) *Self-efficacy in Changing Societies*. New York: Cambridge University Press.

Baron-Cohen, S. (1997) *Mindblindness: An Essay on Autism and the Theory of Mind*. Cambridge, MA: MIT Press.

Bergemann, R. (2013) *An Asperger Leader's Guide to Living and Leading Change*. London: Jessica Kingsley Publishers.

Brandt, T. (2007) *Basics Tendering*. Basel: Birkhäuser Verlag AG.

Brandstätter, H. (1997) 'Becoming an entrepreneur: A question of personality structure?' *Journal of Economic Psychology, 18*, 2–3, 157–177.

Cantillon, R. (2001) *Essay on the Nature of Commerce in General (Classics in Economics)*. New Jersey: Transaction Publishers.

Chell, E., Haworth, J.M. and Brearley, S. (1991) *The Entrepreneurial Personality: Concepts, Cases, and Categories*. Andover, United Kingdom: Cengage Learning EMEA.

Collins, C.J., Hanges, P.J. and Locke, E.A. (2004) *The Relationship of Achievement Motivation to Entrepreneurial Behavior: A Meta-analysis* [Electronic version]. Available at www.digitalcommons.ilr.cornell.edu/articles/831. Accessed 4 January 2014.

Drucker, P.F. (1985) *Innovation and Entrepreneurship:Practice and Principles*. New York: Harper and Row.

Gartner, W.B. (1988) '"Who is an entrepreneur?" is the wrong question.' *American Journal of Small Business 12*, 4, 11–32.

Knight, F. (2006) *Risk, Uncertainty and Profit*. New York: Dover Publications.

Lewis, H. (2012) *Bids, Tenders and Proposals: Winning Business Through Best Practice*. London: Kogan Page.

McClelland, D.C. (1961) *The Achieving Society*. New York: Free Press.

McGuinness, M. (2013) *Resilience: Facing Down Rejection and Criticism on the Road to Success*. London: Lateral Action Books.

Murray, D., Lesser, M. and Lawson, W. (2005) 'Attention, monotropism and the diagnostic criteria for autism.' *Autism 9*, 2, 139–156.

Oxford University (2010) *Oxford English Dictionary*. Oxford: Oxford University Press.

Rauch, A. and Frese, M. (2000) 'Psychological Approaches to Entrepreneurial Success: A General Model and an Overview of Findings.' In C.L. Cooper and I.T. Robertson (eds) *International Review of Industrial and Organizational Psychology* (Vol. 15). New York: John Wiley & Sons Ltd.

Rauch, A. and Frese, M. (2007) 'Born to be an Entrepreneur? Revisiting the Personality Approach to Entrepreneurship.' In J.R. Baum, M. Frese and R. Baron (eds) *The Psychology of Entrepreneurship Research*. Mahwah, NJ: Lawrence Erlbaum Associates.

Pink, D. (2010) *Drive: The Surprising Truth about what Motivates Us*. Edinburgh: Canongate Books.

Rotter, J.B. (1996) 'Generalized expectancies for internal versus external control of reinforcement.' *Psychological Monographs: General and Applied, 80* 1, 1–28.

Schumpeter, J.A. (1935) 'The analysis of economic change.' *Review of Economics and Statistics, 17*, 4, 2–10.

Shane, S.A. and Venkataraman, S. (2000) 'The promise of entrepreneurship as a field of research.' *Academy of Management Review 25*, 1, 217–226.

Index